Series / Number 07-062

D1245386

INFORMATION THEORY

Structural Models for Qualitative Data

KLAUS KRIPPENDORFF
University of Pennsylvania

SAGE PUBLICATIONS
The Publishers of Professional Social Science
Newbury Park London New Delhi

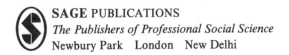

Copyright © 1986 by Sage Publications, Inc.

Printed in the United States of America

All rights reserved. No part of this book may be reproduced or utilized in any form or by any means, electronic or mechanical, including photocopying, recording, or by any information storage and retrieval system, without permission in writing from the publisher.

For information address:

SAGE Publications, Inc.
2111 West Hillcrest Drive
Newbury Park, California 91320

SAGE Publications Ltd.
28 Banner Street
London EC1Y 8QE
England

SAGE Publications India Pvt. Ltd.
M-32 Market
Greater Kailash I
New Delhi 110 048 India

Printed in the United States of America

International Standard Book Number 0-8039-2132-2

Library of Congress Catalog Card No. 86-61611

SECOND PRINTING

When citing a university paper, please use the proper form. Remember to cite the correct Sage University Paper series title and include the paper number. One of the following formats can be adapted (depending on the style manual used):

(1) IVERSEN, GUDMUND R. and NORPOTH, HELMUT (1976) "Analysis of Variance." Sage University Paper series on Quantitative Applications in the Social Sciences, 07-001. Beverly Hills: Sage Pubns.

OR

(2) Iversen, Gudmund R. and Norpoth, Helmut. 1976. *Analysis of Variance*. Sage University Paper series on Quantitative Applications in the Social Sciences, series no. 07-001. Beverly Hills: Sage Pubns.

CONTENTS

Series Editor's Introduction

Professor Krippendorff has written an excellent introduction to information theory, particularly to its application for structural modeling. He provides a lucid discussion of essential topics, such as how to confirm an information theory model, its use in exploratory research, and how it compares with alternative approaches such as network analysis, path analysis, chi-square, and analysis of variance. This places information theory into a framework that most social scientists can readily comprehend and evaluate. Professor Krippendorff's thorough understanding of the theory and use of information theory also takes the careful reader a long way toward competency.

This book is particularly successful at making a rather complicated system for analyzing multivariate qualitative data as simple as possible. Krippendorff does this by building the entire presentation around intuitively appealing notions of information, such as the amount of information provided by an answer to a question, the amount transmitted through a noisy channel, and so on, rather than by using the axioms and theorems of information theory. He also makes copious use of illustrations designed to simplify and clarify the complex issues of structural modeling.

Although this book is an introduction to a well-known but as yet underutilized topic, it does more than merely summarize current knowledge or present basic concepts. It presents new developments, including extensions of classical information theory to many variables, to circular causal processes and to complex models of qualitative data, the use of information theory as an analytical tool, the algebra of information in many variables, and a description of the algorithms needed for computer implementations. Much of Krippendorff's presentation is original and promises wide applications. It should serve equally well as a textbook and as a source book for social scientists and social researchers who are interested in communication explanations and information theory. We recommend it highly to researchers in communication theory, information science, and systems theory, and suggest that it be studied carefully by social scientists interested in structural modeling, particularly in sociology, political science, and psychology. Professor Krippendorff has written his manuscript with these audiences in mind and has succeeded admirably.

—John L. Sullivan
Series Co-Editor

FOREWORD

This volume is motivated by both a renewed interest in qualitative data and recent developments in information theory. Information theory is not merely a convenient statistical tool; it has an additional appeal to social scientists because it provides explanatory structures, theorems of considerable generality, and a powerful calculus for quantities of entropy, information, and communication—all of which are at the root of many social phenomena. The ideas and terminology developed in the first five chapters reflect this dual purpose by providing concepts that are both basic to social theory and introductory to the analytical machinery that follows.

The book's main thesis derives from the extension of the original *Mathematical Theory of Communication* (Shannon and Weaver, 1949) to multiple variables (McGill, 1954; Kullback, 1959; Ashby, 1965, 1969) and to complex structures (Klir, 1976). In particular, this volume treats circular causal or simultaneous dependencies (Krippendorff, 1981) that escaped analysis by most established techniques, as well as penetration by traditional social science theories. The availability of electronic computers played an important role in forging these developments by relieving researchers of routine calculations and allowing them to adopt more powerful conceptualizations governing data analysis and exploration. Finally, multivariate information theory has acquired additional foundations in the work by theoretical statisticians, especially by Kullback, Mosteller, Goodman, Fienberg, Bishop, and others who linked these notions to the ongoing revolution in contingency table analysis, variance analysis, log-linear modeling, and Markov processes in particular.

Although there are many modern facets of information theory, this book presents only what is needed to search for and test structural models of qualitative data; that is, models that exhibit complex relations among their component parts and rely on these relations to interpret given data. Communication or information transmission is just one attractive interpretation of such relationships. In this respect the book's aim is primarily practical, providing tools rather than theorems. It starts with deliberate slowness. Chapters progressively build upon each other. The apparently independent Chapters 6 through 12 are tied together in Chapters 13 through 15. A List of Symbols concludes the book. Readers can develop their own sense of closure even before getting to the end of the volume.

Information Theory is written for advanced undergraduate and and multivariate techniques courses. It should also be of interest to experienced social scientists who can afford to read more selectively. Communication researchers, information scientists, and systems theorists might find these structural models particularly close to their theoretical concerns.

I am grateful for many valuable comments and suggestions received from colleagues, especially from Roger C. Conant, Alexander von Eye, Seth Finn, an anonymous reviewer, and from students at The Annenberg School of Communications, University of Pennsylvania, who used earlier drafts as a text. Finally, the work is unthinkable without W. Ross Ashby's early influence.

INFORMATION THEORY
Structural Models for Qualitative Data

KLAUS KRIPPENDORFF
University of Pennsylvania

1. QUALITATIVE DATA

Qualitative data arise from distinctions drawn within a sample of observations. The act of drawing distinctions makes the observations distinguished of a different kind. No quantitative (ordinal or magnitudinal) differences are implied. Figure 1 depicts distinctions drawn by the *New York Times Magazine* (March 11, 1979) within 4,764 murder cases tried in Florida between 1973 and 1979. Each dot represents a case, and one may notice the conspicuous absence of death sentences for white convicts when the victim is black. Observations may be people, as in Figure 1, but they may also be messages, events, things, processes, anything individually describable, and any motivation to find differences between them qualifies as a basis of drawing distinctions. There may be numerous distinctions. For example, individuals might be classified by occupation, place of birth, sex, party affiliation, marital status, religion, criminal record, psychopathology, telephone number, types of people friendly with, personality type, languages spoken, magazines subscribed to, messages received, media use habits, type of car owned, reasons for visiting a physician, or drugs used—but none of them implies a continuum, and all are logically independent of each other.

Qualitative data are also called *nominal* because the descriptions used are like names, making observations merely same or different without recognizing degrees (e.g., the use of social security numbers); *categorical* because observations are considered by their kind, category, or class to which they belong; *discrete* because the boundaries make and mark a discontinuity in space; and *freely permutable* because the arrangement of observations is arbitrary and conveys no information. The latter is also connoted by the label *unordered* data.

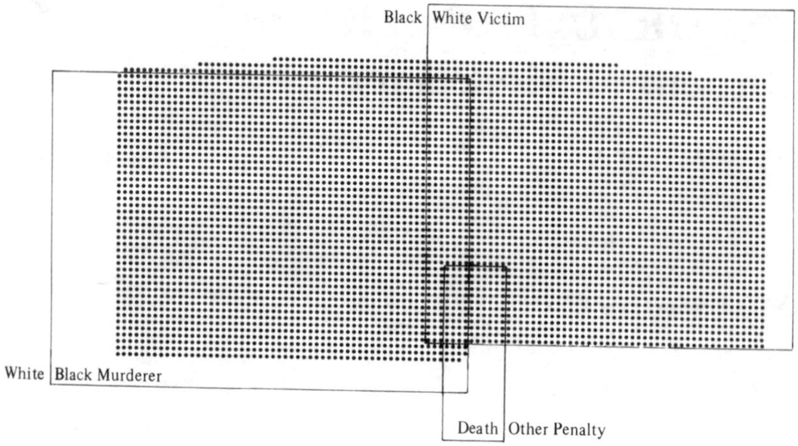

Figure 1

Although many social science data are of this kind, the social sciences are not limited to qualitative data—consider such variables as age, income, time spent watching TV, and intelligence quotient, which are called quantitative because there can be more or less of it. Nor are qualitative data excluded from other fields of inquiry—consider the distinction between gaseous, fluid, and solid states of matter in physics; positions of a relay or the states of a whole switching network in electrical engineering; treatment histories of patients in medicine; genetic structures in biology; and market compositions in economics, all of which are differentiated by kind, not by magnitude. Qualitative data are sometimes considered primitive, but it is their basic nature that makes them probably the most universally available. Qualitative data are found particularly when natural language enters the observations of interest or when a culture or its social institutions prescribe in which categories people, messages, events, products, or procedures are to be viewed, discussed, or responded to.

Qualitative data may come in the form of a protocol of events observed over time, as shown by the interaction sequences in Figure 2. They may be grouped into classes, ignoring time, as in Figure 1, or tabulated by kind, as in Figure 3 (taken from Lipset et al., 1954: 1161).

Distinctions that are drawn independently of each other are said to constitute different *variables.* A variable is a conceptual device comprising an exhaustive set of mutually exclusive *categories* or *values.* The product of these variables constitutes *discrete multivariate* spaces. Figure 4 spatially depicts the data in Figure 1. Herein the three (logically independent) distinctions or variables serve as the dimensions of a space whose $2 \times 2 \times 2$ or eight cells contain the number of cases that these

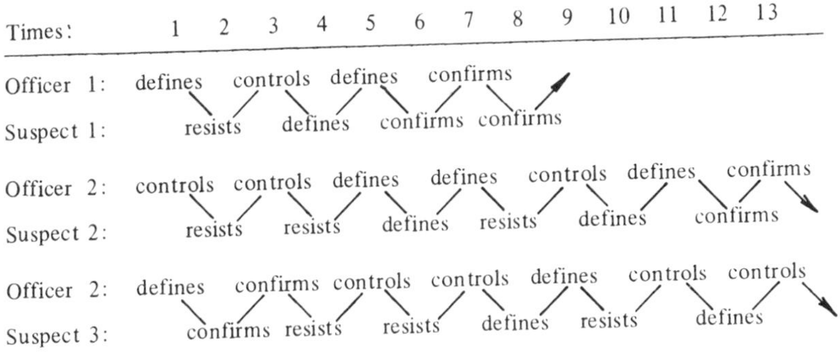

Times:	1	2	3	4	5	6	7	8	9	10	11	12	13

Officer 1:   defines   controls   defines   confirms

Suspect 1:   resists   defines   confirms   confirms

Officer 2:   controls   controls   defines   defines   controls   defines   confirms

Suspect 2:   resists   resists   defines   resists   defines   confirms

Officer 2:   defines   confirms   controls   controls   defines   controls   controls

Suspect 3:   confirms   resists   resists   defines   resists   defines

Figure 2

First Interview	Second Interview	
R +	R +	卌 IIII
R +	R −	III
R +	D +	I
R +	D −	II
R −	R +	卌 卌 I
R −	R −	卌 卌 卌 卌 UI
R −	D +	
R −	D −	I
D +	R +	I
D +	R −	
D +	D +	卌 卌 II
D +	D −	卌 卌 I
D −	R +	I
D −	R −	I
D −	D +	II
D −	D −	卌 卌 卌 卌 卌 卌 卌 卌 卌 卌 卌 卌 卌 UI

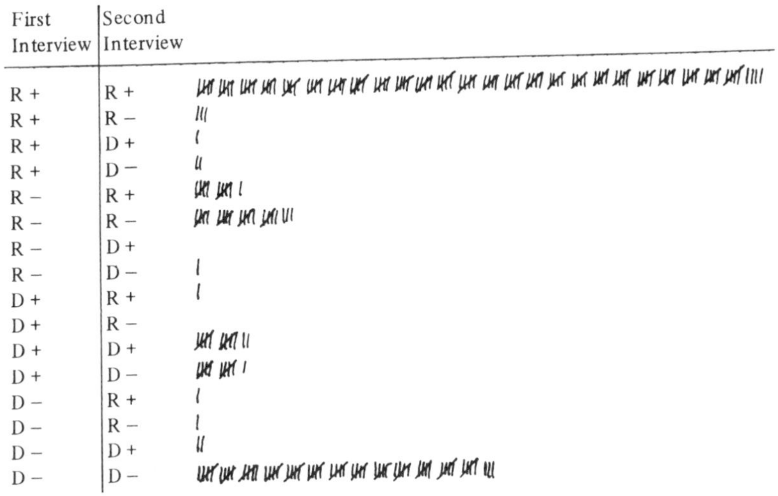

Party Affiliation: Republican (R) or Democrat (D)
In Favor (+) or Against (−) Presidential Candidate Willkie

Figure 3

distinctions regard as of the same kind. Incidentally, the term *count data* reflects this somewhat less important convenience of representing by their number the observations that a *classification scheme* no longer distinguishes. Spatial representations can aid the recognition of patterns in qualitative data (see Figure 44 as an example of where the above may lead to) but become easily incomprehensible when more than three dimensions are involved. *Cross-tabulations* list the frequencies or probabilities of observations in *tabular* or *matrix* form, either breaking a multivariate space into separate subspaces or combining dimensions to obtain comprehensive tables. The latter is exemplified in Figure 5 by

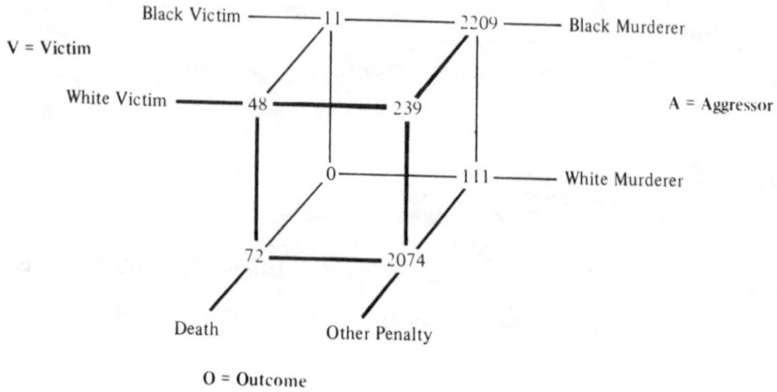

Figure 4

		Time 2			
Exposure to Violent Programming: E → ↓		+		–	
Displayed Aggression:	A → ↓	+	–	+	–
Time 1 +	+	57	9	15	1
	–	10	41	4	15
Time 1 –	+	21	2	37	11
	–	2	15	5	59

Figure 5

four-dimensional panel data, provided to Paul Lazarsfeld by NBC, showing exposure to violent TV programming, E, and aggressive behavior, A, both recorded at two different points in time (Lazarsfeld, 1974).

Our definition of qualitative data *excludes* situations in which (1) distinctions are *vacuous* (i.e., they do not distinguish among observations), thus leaving all of them of the same kind; (2) distinctions are *incomplete* (i.e., they are not drawn among all observations, whether because qualities are partially unknown or categories are ambiguous, fuzzy, or inappropriate), thus rendering some observations incomparable; and (3) the observations distinguished *differ in magnitudes* (i.e., there is an order, a continuum, or a metric underlying the observations).

Notationally, we shall reserve capital letters A, B, C,..., Z, excepting a few found in the List of Symbols, to denote variables and small letters a, b, c,..., z for the qualities or categories constituting them. AB denotes a product of two variables, usually conceived of as a matrix whose rows and columns are labeled $a \epsilon A$ and $b \epsilon B$, respectively, and whose cells are designated by $ab \epsilon AB$. By extension, cross-tabulations or multivariate spaces of an indefinite but finite dimensionality will be referred to by ABC...Z and its cells by $abc \ldots z \epsilon ABC \ldots Z$. In these terms Figure 5 is an $EA \times E'A'$ matrix of 16 eae'a' cells.

2. SELECTIVE INFORMATION

Information is the key to our approach. Although we subsequently will revise this concept to meet the requirements of structural models of qualitative data, to begin with we define information as a measure of the *amount of selective work* a message enables its receiver to do.

Accordingly, asking a yes-or-no question admits an initial uncertainty about what the correct answer might be, and the answer to such a question informs the questioner in the sense of "selecting" one of the two options he or she had in mind, thus removing the initial uncertainty. The answer to a yes-or-no question is taken to convey one *bit* of information which constitutes our basic unit of measurement. To capture this intuition, *uncertainty* U is defined by the dual or base-2 logarithm of the number N of options available. With reference to some variable A,

$$U(A) = \log_2 N_A \qquad [2.1]$$

Accordingly, our yes-or-no question implies $N_A = 2$ logical alternatives and represents $\log_2 2 = 1$ bit of uncertainty.

Given that N refers to logical possibilities, each being of equal weight, U may be said to measure the *logical variety* in a descriptive system of categories. The attribute "logical" is important, as my definition of information does not yet extend to data, frequencies, or observational probabilities. Figure 6 lists some integer values.

The amount of *information* a message—say, a—of the set of possible messages A conveys then becomes the *difference between two states of uncertainty*, the uncertainty U(A) before or without knowledge of that message and the uncertainty U(a) after or with knowledge of that message:

$$I(a \epsilon A) = U(A) - U(a) = \log_2 N_A - \log_2 N_a \qquad [2.2]$$

So if a decision maker must pick one of $N_A = 8$ alternative courses of action and is given a report that shows that six of them lead to certain

Number of Options	Bits	Logical Probability of Options
1	0	1.
2	1	.5
4	2	.25
8	3	.125
16	4	.0625
32	5	.03125
64	6	.015625
128	7	.0078125
256	8	.00390625
512	9	.001953125
1024	10	.0009765625
⋮	⋮	⋮
N	$\log_2 N$	$\frac{1}{N}$

Figure 6

failure, there remain $N_a = 8 - 6 = 2$ options to choose from, making the report worth

$$I(\text{Report}) = U_{\text{before}} - U_{\text{after}} = \log_2 8 - \log_2 2 = 2 \text{ bits}$$

of information, which is equivalent to receiving the answers to two yes-or-no questions. To remove the remaining uncertainty, the decision maker will have to gather one more bit of information or risk a 50% chance of failure. This risk is, of course, considerably less than the risk that existed before receiving the report.

The connection between uncertainty and the risk involved in making wrong decisions leads to an expression of information as a function of the probability of selecting the desired set of alternatives by chance:

$$I(a \epsilon A) = \log_2 N_A - \log_2 N_a = -\log_2 \frac{N_a}{N_A} = -\log_2 P_a \qquad [2.3]$$

where $P_a = N_a/N_A$ is the logical probability of the alternatives in a relative to A. In this algebraically equivalent form, information is seen as a measure of the *difficulty of making appropriate* (to a degree better than chance) *decisions*, and because a less expected message is more informative, information also can be interpreted as a measure of the *surprise value* of a message.

Figure 6 suggests that bits are nothing but a different way of counting options, by the exponents of the value 2 rather than by their number. This use of logarithms makes bits additive when options are multiplicative (see "log" in the List of Symbols). So when P_a is the probability of guessing the answer to question A and P_b is the probability of guessing the answer to an *independent* question B, the probability of guessing both correctly will be $P_{ab} = P_aP_b$.

$$\begin{aligned} \mathbf{I}(ab\epsilon AB) &= -\log_2 P_{ab} \\ &= -\log_2 P_aP_b \\ &= -\log_2 P_a - \log_2 P_b \\ &= \mathbf{I}(a\epsilon A) + \mathbf{I}(b\epsilon B) \end{aligned} \qquad [2.4]$$

It is this property that assures the additivity of information quantities—for example, that two floppy disks can contain twice as much information as one. For further explanations of these ideas, see Krippendorff (1975).

3. ENTROPY, DIVERSITY, VARIETY

Entropy is a measure of *observational variety* or of actual (as opposed to logically possible) diversity. Unlike the measure of selective information, entropy takes into account that messages or categories of events may occur with unequal frequencies or probabilities. The two measures are related, however, and one will be derived from the other.

Reconsider the data in Figure 1. When all n = 4,764 murder cases are considered unique (as they no doubt are from the perspective of the individuals involved), the total amount of uncertainty as to which case we are referring to is $\log_2 4764 = 12.218$ bits. After drawing distinctions suitable to an analysis and thereby putting several observations into one category on grounds that in some crucial respect they are the same, as seen in Figure 4, some uncertainty will be lost. The uncertainty lost by lumping 111 cases into one category is $\log_2 111$; in another it is $\log_2 2074\ldots$; and in the generic a^{th} category of the variable A it is $\mathbf{U}(a) = \log_2 n_a$. On average, this uncertainty is 10.660 bits. A reasonable measure of the uncertainty remaining after such a multiple classification is the difference between the uncertainty in the sample before any classification and the average uncertainty such a classification loses. The resulting measure is called *entropy* **H**. Without loss of generality, it is stated here for one variable (even so, our example could be seen as involving three):

$$H(A) = \log_2 n - \sum_{a \epsilon A} \frac{n_a}{n} (\log_2 n_a) \qquad [3.1]$$

Whereas the selective information in 2.3 quantifies a simple reduction in logical possibilities, the entropy in 3.1 quantifies a reduction of n distinct observations to fewer categories. In our example, the entropy is 12.218 – 10.660 = 1.558 bits. By rearranging the parts of 3.1, the entropy can be seen to be the average amount of information required to select (predict or identify) observations by categories:

$$H(A) = \sum_{a \epsilon A} \frac{n_a}{n} \left(-\log_2 \frac{n_a}{n}\right) \qquad [3.2]$$

By replacing the relative frequency n_a/n with its limiting case, the probability p_a, we obtain:

$$H(A) = -\sum_{a \epsilon A} p_a \log_2 p_a \qquad [3.3]$$

which is the most familiar definition of entropy and was introduced in this form by Shannon and Weaver (1949). (Although there are occasions on which the relative frequencies in a sample deviate from the probabilities in the population from which that sample was drawn, we will be concerned with this difference only when testing the significance of information quantities and will use relative frequencies and probabilities interchangeably otherwise.) In the one-variable "outcomes of murder trials" there are a subtotal of 131 death convictions that are much more difficult to guess ($-\log_2 p_{\text{death penalty}}$ = 5.184 bits) than the 4,633 other outcomes ($-\log_2 p_{\text{other}}$ = .0402 bits). Considering the different weights imposed by their rather unequal frequency of occurrence, $-p_{\text{death penalty}}\log_2 p_{\text{death penalty}}$ = .1426 and $-p_{\text{other}}\log_2 p_{\text{other}}$ = .0391, the entropy in this distinction sums to .1817 bits, quantitatively reflecting a rather predictable outcome.

Part of the definition of entropy, and one reason for calling it a measure of observational variety, is that unobserved possibilities do not enter the measure. The average is computed only for categories of observations that do occur at least once. This is reflected in the convention adopted here: $0\log_2 0 = 0$.

Note some of its properties. Entropies are *zero or positive* and *limited by*

$$0 \leqslant H(A) \leqslant H(A)_{max} = \log_2(\min[N_A, n]) \qquad [3.4]$$

where N_A is the number of categories in variable A and n is the sample size. The entropy is zero when observational variety is absent—that is, when distinctions are vacuous and all observations are of the same kind, $p_a = 1$ for one category and zero for all others, in which case both $1\log_2 1 = 0$ and by convention $0\log_2 0 = 0$. The entropy is maximum when the N_A cells are occupied either by the same number of observations, $n_a = n/N_A$, in which case frequencies and probabilities are uniformly distributed, or by $n_a = 1$ at most, in which case all observations are unique. Thus the amount of uncertainty (2.1) is a limiting condition for quantities of entropy. In the example, the victims' race, with its almost uniform distribution of 51% and 49%, measures an entropy of .9997 bits and is near its maximum of 1 bit.

Entropies do not respond to the nature of the categories involved. Their labels are freely permutable. Only the set of frequencies or probabilities matters. It is in this sense that entropies are said to be *content-free*. What is true for the arrangement of values in a variable is also true for the arrangement of cells in a matrix or space of greater dimensionality. The entropy

$$H(ABC..Z) = -\sum_{a \epsilon A}\sum_{b \epsilon B} \cdots \sum_{z \epsilon Z} p_{abc..z} \log_2 p_{abc..z} \qquad [3.5]$$

which is an obvious generalization of 3.3, reflects more and finer distinctions than those drawn by any single variable, but it too measures nothing other than a dimensionless collection of frequencies or probabilities.

Unlike variance measures of deviations from a mean which make sense only for unimodel distributions, entropies assume nothing about the nature of the frequency or probability distribution they assess and are thus *non-parametric* measures of variety and entirely general in this respect.

Entropies are averages. Figure 7 illustrates how one might interpret classification. This partition of 32 events measures 1.875 bits. The decision tree recursively divides these events into equal parts, each amounting to 1 bit. However, after the first distinction, the second is made in only half of the cases and thus contributes only .5 bits to the measure. The third distinction is made in only a quarter of the cases and contributes .25 bits, and so on. These four contributions add to the total of 1.875 bits, QED. It follows that 1 bit of entropy may reflect not only two equally likely alternatives but could also arise from decisions among

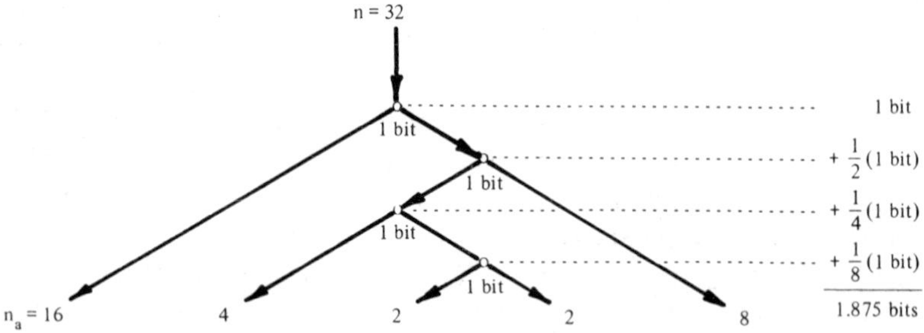

Figure 7

more than two rather unlikely cases. Figure 8 exemplifies several distributions, all of which measure approximately 1 bit.

Entropies are a function of relative magnitudes, probabilities being the most common form. The sample size does not influence the entropy values (except in the form of a statistical bias, which will be considered later). Entropies may be *standardized* or expressed relative to their maximum:

$$0 \leqslant \frac{H(A)}{H(A)_{max}} \leqslant 1 \qquad [3.6]$$

Standardized or relative entropies no longer express the magnitude of diversity or variety (analogous to variance) but may be interpreted as an index of uniformity (analogous to the standard deviation). Entropy measures provide access to a rich source of data for the construction of theories in which variety, diversity, and differentiation are the target of generalizations. For example, early studies in psychology of absolute judgments led to generalizations of human information-processing limits over several sensory domains (Miller, 1956; Attneave, 1959). The entropy of prose (Shannon and Weaver, 1949; Weltner, 1973) has been correlated with readability (Taylor, 1953, 1956), with English proficiency (Darnell, 1970, 1972), and with reader enjoyment (Finn, 1985). Similar intentions led to applications of entropy measures to art and aesthetics (Bense, 1956; Attneave, 1959; Moles, 1966; Berlyne, 1971), newspapers (Schramm, 1955), television programming (Watt and Krull, 1974; Watt and Welch, 1983), and to the instrumental and functional complexity of cultural objects (Moles, 1960).

To test whether the press fulfills its promise of keeping the public informed, Chaffee and Wilson (1977) used entropies to measure the diversity of public opinion in media-poor and media-rich environments. Danowski (1974) and Danowski and Ruchinskas (1979) correlated the entropy of media exposure with aging and with the complexity of

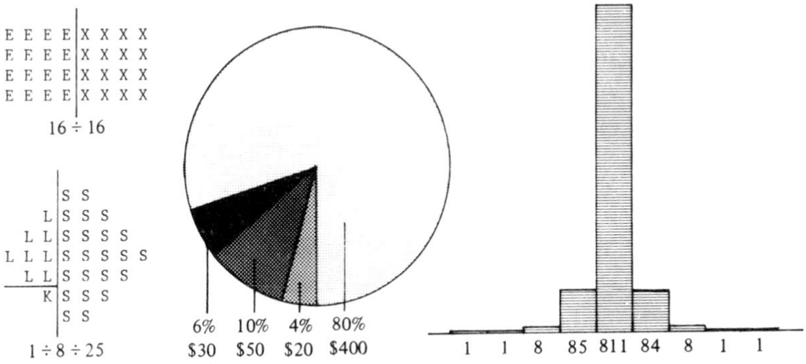

Figure 8

interpersonal networks. Entropy is also the primary target of what has become known as the convergence model of communication (Rogers and Kincaid, 1981). It suggests that communication processes change the distributions of beliefs, values, and behaviors within a population and reverse the natural tendency toward increasing entropy.

Entropy is also the target of many processes of social control. For example, political succession can be seen as reducing the great variety of aspirants to a political office until the last uncertainty is removed by ballot. In a pedagogical example, Lachman, Lachman, and Butterfield (1979) cite an entropy of nearly 4 bits from November 1975 data on the probable success of some 17 candidates for the U.S. presidency. The preelection process reduced this entropy to nearly 1 bit (characterizing the nearly equally likely success of Carter and Ford before election day on which voters removed the remaining uncertainty).

Finally, entropy is also the key to a fundamental law in the cybernetics of regulation. Ashby's (1956) law of requisite variety, which states that "only variety can destroy variety," implies that the survival of a system depends on its ability to generate at least as much variety within its boundaries as exists in the form of threatening disturbances from its environment. In light of such a fundamental condition, many entropy measures gain social importance. For example, Theil (1972) reported studies measuring occupational diversity in cities, industrial concentration in the United States, and the entropies of employment, markets, income, and political representation, all of which can be linked to the growth and decline of social systems. Montroll (1983) applied the entropy function to Sears catalogues and showed that the company's success depended on keeping variations in the entropy of prices nearly constant. Galtung (1975) related entropy to a general theory of peace.

Subsequent chapters take the wide applicability of entropy measures for granted, avoid using them as measures or indices in their own right, and focus instead on the analytical opportunities they offer, Shannon's theory of communication being an early recognition of these.

4. SHANNON'S THEORY OF COMMUNICATION

Shannon's widely publicized model of communication (Shannon and Weaver, 1949) is a chain of processes as shown in Figure 9. The model is of considerable generality. The labels on its boxes do not matter but merely exemplify one interpretation. The model is applicable not only to mediated communication (e.g., telephone, newsprint, computers) but also to the flow of orders through a chain of command, to the sequential analysis of data in the course of a scientific experiment, or to information processing within an organism. What is important is that each of these boxes is described by a transformation, with variable inputs, variable outputs, and transition probabilities connecting the two. A transformation so described is also called a *code*. Shannon's theory keeps track of information flows through such coding processes, quantifies channel capacities, redundancies, and errors, and offers various theorems relating them.

To understand any one of Shannon's boxes in this chain, we must identify two sets of categories, whether they be signals, messages, judgments, courses of action, types of contents, or patterns in the input or output. We must then ascertain the connections between them. Figure 10 gives four such examples sagittally and tabularly. In a *Perfect Channel*, the messages sent and the messages received correspond one to one. They do not need to be the same—as in translations or in sound recordings—as long as they are not irrecoverably mixed. In a perfect channel of communication, encoding and decoding are inverses of each other. Imperfect channels entail two kinds of errors: noise and equivocation.

Noise and Equivocation

Noise occurs when a sender cannot be certain about how the message is received. In Figure 10 this is indicated by branching arrows or by two

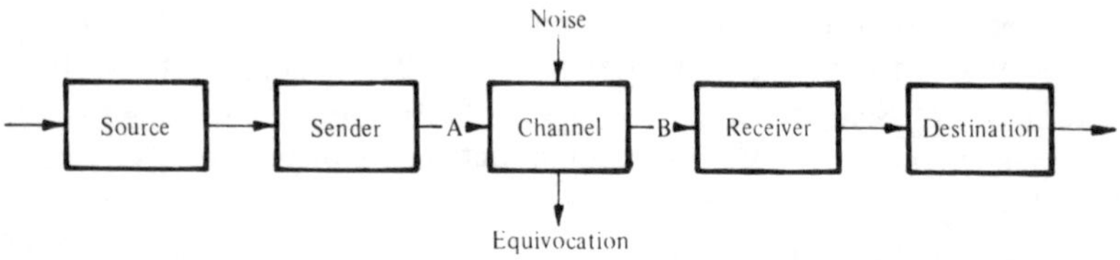

Figure 9

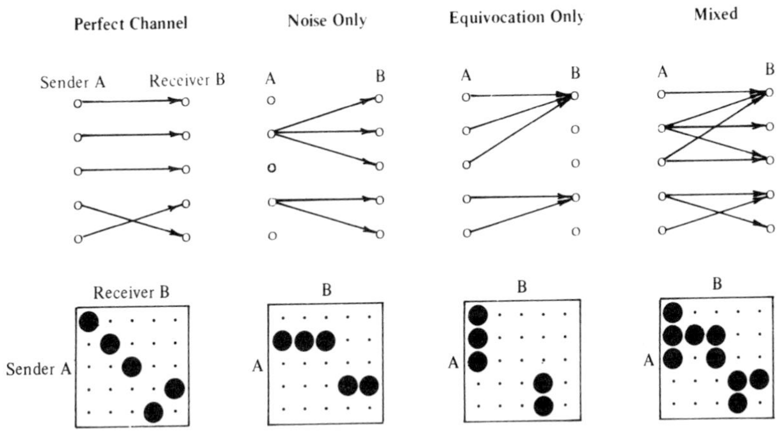

Figure 10

or more entries per row. The term is borrowed from acoustical experiences in telephone communication that make hearing difficult and is generalized here to refer to all unexplainable variation, including the static on a TV screen and incomprehensible rhetoric. Noise need not be undesirable as in creative pursuits or in political discourse, in which ambiguity may be intentional. Noise simply measures the input-unrelated variety in an output stream.

Equivocation occurs when the receiver is unable to differentiate between two or more messages sent. In Figure 10 this is indicated by converging arrows or by two or more entries per column. Equivocation can be taken to mean "regarded as equal" and occurs not only when a receiver cannot make out which message was intended but in all efforts to classify, abbreviate, simplify, or abstract. Equivocation measures the variety removed from the input stream.

The mathematical machinery for analyzing such situations requires data on either (a) the probabilities or frequencies with which messages are sent plus the transition probabilities of how each sent message is received, (b) the probabilities or frequencies with which messages are received plus the (inverse transition) probabilities of how each received message was sent, or, finally, (c) the probabilities or frequencies of all transitions between or cooccurrences of values from two or more variables. Figure 11 defines the relevant probabilities and frequencies in terms of (c). (For notational simplicity we are now taking for granted a's membership in A, b's membership in B, and so on and drop references to relative frequencies in preference to probabilities where practical.)

According to 3.2 and 3.3, the sender's entropy in the vertical margin (row sums) in Figure 11 is

$$\mathbf{H}(A) = -\sum_a p_a \log_2 p_a = -\sum_a \frac{n_a}{n} \log_2 \frac{n_a}{n}$$

The receiver's entropy in the horizontal margin (column sums) is

$$\mathbf{H}(B) = -\sum_b p_b \log_2 p_b = -\sum_b \frac{n_b}{n} \log_2 \frac{n_b}{n}$$

and the total entropy in the table of cooccurrences is

$$\mathbf{H}(AB) = -\sum_a \sum_b p_{ab} \log_2 p_{ab} = -\sum_a \sum_b \frac{n_{ab}}{n} \log_2 \frac{n_{ab}}{n}$$

Without reference to marginal entropies, **H**(AB)'s *absolute limits* are as in 3.4, and *with* reference to marginal entropies, **H**(AB)'s *relative limits* are

$$\max[\mathbf{H}(A), \mathbf{H}(B)] \leqslant \mathbf{H}(AB) \leqslant \mathbf{H}(A) + \mathbf{H}(B) \qquad [4.1]$$

In 4.1 the minimum entropy represents the case in which either the rows or the columns of the transition matrix have no more than one non-zero entry each, the corresponding conditional probabilities are unity, and the relation manifest in this distribution is many-to-one. The perfect channel in Figure 10 exemplifies the extreme case of this condition, a one-to-one relation. Much of the beauty of Shannon's information calculus rests on the fact that the maximum entropy in a matrix is the sum of the two marginal entropies. We noted this property in 2.4. Now 4.1 implies that the probabilities $\pi_{ab} = p_a p_b$ of this maximum entropy distribution need not be computed explicitly.

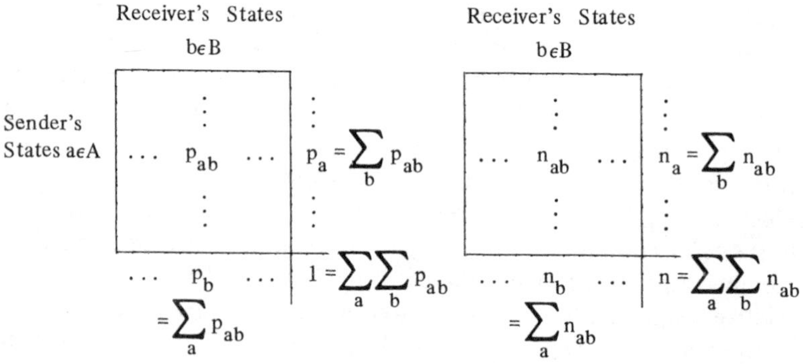

Figure 11

The *amount of noise* is variously defined by

$$\mathbf{H}_A(B) = \mathbf{H}(AB) - \mathbf{H}(A) \qquad [4.2]$$

$$= \sum_a p_a \, \mathbf{H}_a(B)$$

$$= \sum_a p_a \left[-\sum_b p_{b|a} \log_2 p_{b|a} \right]$$

$$= \sum_a \frac{n_a}{n} \left[-\sum_b \frac{n_{ab}}{n_a} \log_2 \frac{n_{ab}}{n_a} \right]$$

that is, as the algebraic difference between the joint entropy **H**(AB) and the sender's entropy **H**(A), as the average of the entropies $\mathbf{H}_a(B)$ in the rows of Figure 11, the latter being expressed either in terms of conditional probabilities $p_{b|a}$ or relative frequencies n_{ab}/n_a. If each message were received as one and only one message, then transition probabilities $p_{b|a} = 0$ or 1, all row entropies $\mathbf{H}_a(B) = 0$, $\mathbf{H}(AB) = \mathbf{H}(B)$, and noise is absent. Positive quantities of noise therefore indicate the confusion the known message "a" causes in the receiver B. The *amount of noise* is limited by

$$\max[0, \mathbf{H}(B) - \mathbf{H}(A)] \leqslant \mathbf{H}_A(B) \leqslant \mathbf{H}(B) \leqslant \mathbf{H}(AB) \qquad [4.3]$$

The *amount of equivocation* follows the same logic except that the positions of sender and receiver and, consequently, the references to rows and columns are reversed. If $\mathbf{H}_A(B)$ measures the noise in a communication channel, $\mathbf{H}_B(A)$ becomes its equivocation.

Information Transmitted

The amount of information transmitted through a channel can also be expressed in several conceptually different but mathematically equivalent ways. As the difference between the maximum entropy and the observed entropy,

$$\mathbf{T}(A:B) = \mathbf{H}(A) + \mathbf{H}(B) - \mathbf{H}(AB) \qquad [4.4]$$

as the difference between the receiver's entropy and that part of its entropy which is noise,

$$\mathbf{T}(A:B) = \mathbf{H}(B) - \mathbf{H}_A(B) \qquad [4.5]$$

as the difference between the sender's entropy and that part of its entropy lost by equivocation,

$$\mathbf{T}(A:B) = \mathbf{H}(A) - \mathbf{H}_B(A) \qquad [4.6]$$

and in terms of probabilities or frequencies,

$$\mathbf{T}(A:B) = \sum_a \sum_b p_{ab} \log_2 \frac{p_{ab}}{\pi_{ab}} \qquad [4.7]$$

$$= \sum_a \sum_b p_{ab} \log_2 \frac{p_{ab}}{p_a p_b} = \sum_a \sum_b \frac{n_{ab}}{n} \log_2 \frac{\frac{n_{ab}}{n_a n_b}}{n}$$

The probabilities $\pi_{ab} = p_a p_b$ are expected when sender and receiver do not communicate and operate independently of each other. The so-called maximum entropy probabilities provide the standard against which the observed probabilities p are evaluated explicitly in 4.7 and implicitly in 4.4 through 4.6. The $\log_2 p/\pi$ is also known as the log-likelihood ratio.

The relations among these five measures can be visualized with Figure 12. It depicts the flow of information through any one of the components of a communication chain. Equivocation subtracts from the sender's entropy, yielding the quantity of information actually transmitted, and noise adds unrelated variation to this transmitted quality, yielding the entropy at the receiver. The amount of information transmitted is the entropy shared by both—input and output, sender and receiver, and so on.

The limits of the amount of information transmitted can be shown with 4.4. When **H**(AB) is maximum by 4.1, the difference that defines **T**(A:B) becomes zero. When **H**(AB) is minimum, then the smaller of the two, **H**(A) or **H**(B), remains. Hence:

$$0 \leqslant \mathbf{T}(A:B) \leqslant \mathbf{T}(A:B)_{max} = \min[\mathbf{H}(A), \mathbf{H}(B)] \qquad [4.8]$$

leading to the so-called index of predictability:

$$0 \leqslant \mathbf{t}_{A:B} = \frac{\mathbf{T}(A:B)}{\mathbf{T}(A:B)_{max}} \leqslant 1 \qquad [4.9]$$

We will generalize the maximum amount of information in 8.9 and the index in 13.5.

Inasmuch as the algebraic relations between entropies might elude recognition of the implicit comparisons that are made by this informa-

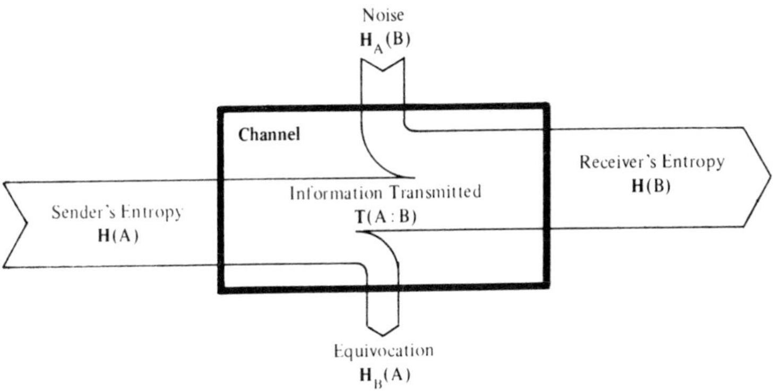

Figure 12

			Second Interview B				
			R+	R−	D+	D−	
First Interview A	Republican for Willkie	R+	129	3	1	2	135
	Republican against Willkie	R−	11	23	0	1	35
	Democrat for Willkie	D+	1	0	12	11	24
	Democrat against Willkie	D−	1	1	2	68	72
			142	27	15	82	266

Figure 13

tion quantity, we apply three alternative computations to the data in Figure 3, now summarized in Figure 13. Although these data are not literally about sending and receiving messages, they do conform to the requirements, particularly to form c. The absence of information transmitted from the first to the second interview would mean that changes occurred at random, whereas non-zero amounts would indicate that attitudes in the second interview are to an extent indicated by T(A:B) predictable from knowledge of the first, the retention of these attitudes offering the most obvious explanation.

Applying 3.3 and 3.5 directly to the table and its margins (using "A" to designate the first interview and "B" the second) yields

$$H(A) = 1.705 \text{ bits}$$
$$H(B) = 1.575 \text{ bits}$$
$$H(AB) = 2.227 \text{ bits}$$

By 4.4, the amount of information transmitted between the two interviews is

$$T(A:B) = H(A) + H(B) - H(AB) = 1.054 \text{ bits}$$

This quantity is statistically significant beyond reasonable doubt, an issue addressed in Chapters 10 and 11. By 4.8, $\mathbf{T}(A{:}B)_{max} = 1.575$ bits, and the difference between the observed and this maximum quantity is the result of some voters changing their minds. These cases are found in the off-diagonal cells of the matrix and constitute noise.

Although this computation of the information quantity is straightforward and simple, it does not shed light on where changes have introduced uncertainties and how they affect the measure. To highlight such analyses, Figure 14 demonstrates a second approach. It shows the computation of the quantity of noise, using 4.2. We see the conditional probabilities $p_{b|a}$ tabulated and the entropies $\mathbf{H}_a(B)$ associated with each row of this matrix. Both respectively exhibit and indicate the results obtained during the second interview given the outcome of the first. The noise $\mathbf{H}_A(B)$ is the average row entropy $\mathbf{H}_a(B)$. In the absence of any pattern across time, we would expect the distribution of conditional probabilities $p_{a|b}$ to replicate the unconditional probabilities p_b, in which case all $\mathbf{H}_a(B) = \mathbf{H}(B)$ and $\mathbf{T}(A{:}B) = 0$. In the other extreme, when the second interview merely replicates the first, all observations would turn up in the diagonal, each row would have only one occupied cell, all $\mathbf{H}_a(B) = 0$ and $\mathbf{T}(A{:}B) = \mathbf{H}(B)$, which is the maximum information retainable in this case. In the example all entropies $\mathbf{H}_a(B)$ are non-zero and smaller than $\mathbf{H}(B)$. We also note that most changes understandably occur in the two rows for the initially conflicting categories (R–) and (D+), which are indicated by an entropy markedly higher than in the rows for the consistent categories, (R+) and (D–). But because the two conflicting categories occur less frequently than the other two, their row entropies also contribute less to the total amount of information in the data (last column in Figure 14). Subtracting the quantity of noise, $\mathbf{H}_A(B)$, from the entropy in the second interview, $\mathbf{H}(B)$, as in 4.5, again yields $\mathbf{T}(A{:}B) = \mathbf{H}(B) - \mathbf{H}_A(B) = 1.575 - .522 = 1.054$ bits of information

	$p_{b\|a}$				p_a	$\mathbf{H}_a(B)$	$p_a\mathbf{H}_a(B)$
a = R+	.956	.022	.007	.015	.507	.327	.166
R–	.314	.657	.000	.029	.132	1.069	.141
D+	.042	.000	.500	.458	.090	1.207	.109
D–	.014	.014	.028	.944	.271	.393	.106

p_b				$\mathbf{H}(B)$	– $\mathbf{H}_A(B)$ =	$\mathbf{T}(A{:}B)$
.534	.102	.056	.308	1.575	.522	1.054

Figure 14

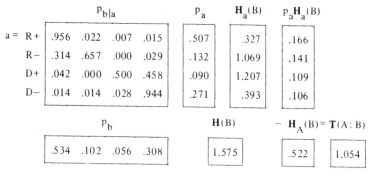

retained between the two interviews. With this simple entropy difference, the quantity implicitly compares the conditional probabilities $p_{b|a}$ with the (unconditional) probabilities p_b row for row.

The third approach to computing information quantities is illustrated by applying 4.7. It compares the observed probabilities p_{ab} with the maximum entropy probabilities π_{ab} that are expected under conditions of independence. Both of these and the weighted log-likelihood ratios are given in Figure 15. In the top and leftmost (R+R+) cell of these matrices we find the observed probability $p_{ab} = 129/266 = .485$ to be larger than the expected probability $\pi_{ab} = p_a p_b = .508 \times .534 = .271$; the latter would have been observed had the attitudes expressed during the two interviews been unrelated or changed at random. In this cell observations exceed expectations by a factor of $p_{ab}/\pi_{ab} = 1.790$. Because this likelihood ratio exceeds unity, the log-likelihood ratio is positive. The weighted log-likelihood ratio contributes $p_{ab}\log_2 p_{ab}/\pi_{ab} = .407$ bits to the total amount of information. Figure 15 shows these contributions for all cells. It turns out that all diagonal cells are positive as well. The signs of the weighted log-likelihood ratios indicate whether observations are above (plus) or below (minus) expectations. The sum over all of these quantities is the amount of information retained between the two interviews, or **T**(A:B) = 1.054 bits as before. Again, regardless of how the amount of information is computed, the resulting quantity expresses the above comparisons implicitly.

p_{ab}

a = R+	.485	.011	.004	.008
R−	.041	.086	.000	.004
D+	.004	.000	.045	.041
D−	.004	.004	.008	.255

$\pi_{ab} = p_a p_b$

.271	.052	.027	.156
.070	.013	.007	.047
.048	.009	.005	.028
.145	.028	.015	.028

$p_{ab} \log_2 \dfrac{p_{ab}}{\pi_{ab}}$

a = R+	.407	−.025	−.011	−.033
R−	−.032	.233		−.013
D+	−.014		.142	.024
D−	−.020	−.011	−.008	.413

1.054 bits
= **T**(A : B)

Figure 15

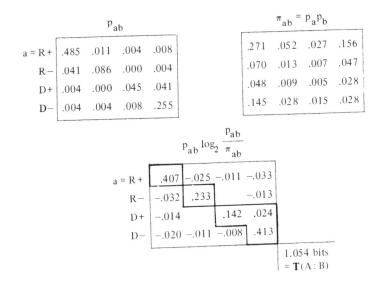

Redundancy

One of Shannon's most celebrated contributions is the proof that noise that detracts from the amount of information otherwise transmittable can be counteracted up to an arbitrarily small error either by additional correction channels of a capacity equal to or exceeding the amount of noise entering the communications or by coding an equivalent amount of redundancy into the channel. Familiar forms of the latter are repetitions of the messages sent or the use of fewer than all possible messages, including parity checks of various complexity. This gives rise to measures of redundancy. For simple entropies within a communication channel, *redundancy* is the difference between the entropy of a uniform distribution and the observed entropy and is an information measure in its own right:

$$T(\bar{A}) = H(A)_{max} - H(A) \qquad [4.10]$$

or expressed as an index:

$$\frac{T(\bar{A})}{H(A)_{max}} = 1 - \frac{H(A)}{H(A)_{max}} \qquad [4.11]$$

The latter led Shannon and Weaver (1949) to observe that the English language is about 50% redundant, a figure that other researchers have upgraded to 70%. This redundancy accounts for the fact that we can detect and correct typographical errors and syntactical mistakes in English prose. A nonredundant language would be a more efficient means of communication but totally insensitive to transmission errors of any kind. For example, this book consists of about 22,000 words and names, and has a word entropy of 8,613 bits, and because it uses only about 2,500 kinds of words, it is 24% redundant.

The total amount of information transmitted can be generalized to many variables (McGill, 1954; Ashby, 1969):

$$T(A:B:C:\ldots:Z) = H(A) + H(B) + H(C) + \ldots + H(Z) - H(ABC\ldots Z) \qquad [4.12]$$

As stated earlier, Shannon's theory was originally concerned with a particular structural model of communication involving binary components (having inputs and outputs only) and no loops. The causal chain in Figure 9 exemplifies this case. Foreshadowing extensions to more complex models in subsequent chapters, the total amount of information in a chain A→B→C→D→…→Z, similar to Figure 9, turns out to be the sum of the transmissions in each of its components:

$$\mathbf{T}(A:B:C:\ldots:Z) = \mathbf{T}(A:B) + \mathbf{T}(B:C) + \mathbf{T}(C:D) + \ldots + \mathbf{T}(Y:Z) \quad [4.13]$$

The model assumes that communication between A and C, A and Z, B and Z, and so on and all higher-order interactions are absent. For such chains a bottleneck theorem states that the amount of information a chain can maximally transmit from its input to its output cannot exceed the amount transmitted by its weakest link:

$$\mathbf{T}(A:Z) \leqslant \min[\mathbf{T}(A:B), \mathbf{T}(B:C), \mathbf{T}(C:D), \ldots, \mathbf{T}(Y:Z)] \quad [4.14]$$

Subsequent chapters expand Shannon's original conceptions.

5. COMPARISONS OF QUALITATIVE VARIATES

Situations may arise in which comparisons of simple *measures* of diversity will not suffice. Recall Figure 8, which depicts rather different distributions of equal entropy. We are concerned here with comparing two frequency or probability *distributions* within the same variables. Consider a hypothetical set of data created after Theil (1972), who studied racial segregation in Chicago with entropy measures.

Figure 16 lists the racial composition in all five schools of a district. The first and largest school is predominantly black. The second is predominantly Caucasian, with the fifth and smallest being nearly exclu-

	Races b of B				
	Black	Caucasian	Hispanic	Asian	Racial Entropy (Bits)
a = 1	422	91	151	0	$\mathbf{H}_1(B) = 1.294$
2	11	257	37	66	$\mathbf{H}_2(B) = 1.292$
3	68	68	68	68	$\mathbf{H}_3(B) = 2.000$
4	50	51	25	14	$\mathbf{H}_4(B) = 1.837$
5	1	98	1	2	$\mathbf{H}_5(B) = .307$
Total	552	565	282	150	$\mathbf{H}(B) = 1.836$

Figure 16

sively so. Although there are apparent differences in the first two schools' composition, both have nearly the same racial entropy of 1.292 bits, which shows that the content-free quantities of entropy by themselves say nothing about differences between two frequency distributions and hence about racial discrimination or bias in this case. Expectations are important. If race does not enter a school's admissions policy, we would expect the racial mixture within each school to resemble that in the school-age population of the surrounding community as a whole. This is clearly not the case in the first, second, and last schools, which have unexpectedly large numbers in one category, or in the third school, which, despite good intentions, employs an equal quota system. We approach such comparisons in two ways.

Informational Distance

One way is suggested by comparing one row with the aggregate sum of all others. In effect this means rearranging the data in Figure 16 into several $2 \times N_B$ matrices as in Figure 17, in our example, one for each school. The amount of information transmitted between the two variables, a versus not-a and B, as obtained by 4.4 through 4.7, measures the dissimilarity or difference between one row and all others and is called the *informational distance* $\mathbf{T}(a\bar{a}\!:\!B)$:

$$\mathbf{T}(a\bar{a} : B) = \sum_b p_{ab} \log_2 \frac{p_{ab}}{p_a p_b} + \sum_b (p_b - p_{ab}) \log_2 \frac{p_b - p_{ab}}{(1 - p_a) p_b} \qquad [5.1]$$

$\mathbf{T}(a\bar{a}\!:\!B)$ is zero or positive. It is maximum if, whenever p_{ab} is zero, $p_b - p_{ab}$ is non-zero and vice versa and cannot exceed 1 bit. It is zero when the probability distribution $p_{a|b}$ in a equals that of $p_{\bar{a}|b}$ in $\bar{a}$, in which case both equal the distribution of p_b in the margin and $p_{ab} = p_a p_b$. This plus the symmetry $\mathbf{T}(a\bar{a}\!:\!B)$ satisfies all requirements of a *distance function*. Measures of this kind have been used in document retrieval and pattern recognition but have also been applied to make qualitative data amenable to multidimensional scaling analyses.

In our example the use of the informational distance $\mathbf{T}(a\bar{a}\!:\!B)$ as a measure of racial discrimination is marred by its otherwise useful symmetry. It responds to the volumes of discriminatory decisions regardless of whether they are made inside a school (first row in Figure 17) or in its aggregate environment (second row in Figure 17). When schools are of rather unequal size, the bias in smaller schools is likely to remain unnoticed in contrast to the lack of differentiation within their then larger environments. For example, the informational distance

	1	. . .	$b \epsilon B$	. . .	N_B	
$a \epsilon A$		. . .	p_{ab}	. . .		$p_a = \sum_b p_{ab}$
$\bar{a} \epsilon A$		. . .	$p_b - p_{ab}$	. . .		$1 - p_a$
		. . .	p_b	. . .		1

Figure 17

between the second school and its environment is .185 bits, whereas for the last school, which is in fact more selective, it is only .081 bits.

Informational Bias

The second measure compares observed and expected probabilities as well but only within any one row (or column, as appropriate). The *informational bias*

$$\mathbf{T}(a:B) = \frac{1}{p_a} \sum_b p_{ab} \log_2 \frac{p_{ab}}{p_a p_b} \qquad [5.2]$$

consists of only the first part of $\mathbf{T}(a\bar{a}:B)$ in 5.1. Observations in this a^{th} row have the status of a subsample, and $\mathbf{T}(a:B)$ measures the degree to which that subsample differs from the whole sample of which it is a part. In the algebraically equivalent forms,

$$\mathbf{T}(a:B) = \sum_b p_{b|a} \log_2 \frac{p_{b|a}}{p_b} = -\sum_b p_{b|a} \log_2 p_b - \mathbf{H}_a(B)$$

the measure appears to be the difference between an entropy in B, which is weighted not by p_b, as in $\mathbf{H}(B)$, but by $p_{b|a}$, and the (conditional) entropy $\mathbf{H}_a(B)$ in the ath row. $\mathbf{T}(a:B)$ is related to the total amount of information in a matrix by

$$\mathbf{T}(A:B) = \sum_a \sum_b p_{ab} \log_2 \frac{p_{ab}}{p_a p_b} = \sum_a p_a \, \mathbf{T}(a:B)$$

and to $\mathbf{T}(a\bar{a}:B)$ by

$$\mathbf{T}(a\bar{a}:B) = p_a \, \mathbf{T}(a:B) + p_{\bar{a}} \, \mathbf{T}(\bar{a}:B)$$

Obviously, the informational bias is not symmetrical regarding the two distributions, $\mathbf{T}(a:B) \neq \mathbf{T}(\bar{a}:B)$, and therefore cannot be interpreted as a distance function.

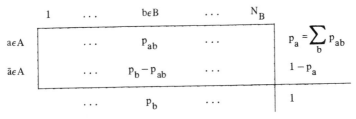

	$p_{b\|a}$				$-\sum_b p_{b\|a} \log_2 p_b$	$-$ $\mathbf{H}_a(B)$	$=$ $\mathbf{T}(a:B)$
a = 1	.636	.137	.227	.000	1.701	1.294	.407
2	.029	.693	.100	.178	1.896	1.292	.604
3	.250	.250	.250	.250	2.187	2.000	.187
4	.357	.364	.179	.100	1.837	1.837	.000
5	.010	.959	.010	.021	1.505	.307	1.198

p_b				$\mathbf{H}(B)$	$-$ $\mathbf{H}_A(B)$	$=$ $\mathbf{T}(A:B)$
.357	.363	.183	.097	1.836	1.405	.431

Figure 18

For the racial segregation data, Figure 18 lists the conditional probabilities $p_{b|a}$, the probabilities p_b to which the former are compared, and the entropy components leading to $\mathbf{T}(a:B)$ to the right of this matrix.

Informational bias measures reveal, what is intuitively rather obvious, that the last school follows the most stringent discriminatory policy, making, on average, more than one decision per student to keep certain racial groups out. All of these measures except for the fourth school are significant beyond reasonable doubt.

Bias measures of this kind have many applications and will be generalized in Chapter 13 for examining strata in complex models.

6. STRUCTURAL MODELS

Generally a model is intended to represent a portion of reality so as to explain, to predict, or to control certain features of that reality which are otherwise difficult to observe or to manage. Here the "reality" of interest is manifest in multivariate qualitative data. Any model of such data must be specified by a limited number of parameters with respect to which the model and the data correspond. Given this limited correspondence, a model must then be able to generate a set of artificial or hypothetical data within the original multivariate space, and if the two sets of data match or their difference is insignificant, one is justified to conclude that the model explains, accounts for, simulates, or replicates the data in hand. Figure 19 illustrates what is involved. The approach taken here is traceable to Ashby's (1964) constraint analysis and has recently been termed "reconstructability analysis" (Klir, 1981). We pre-

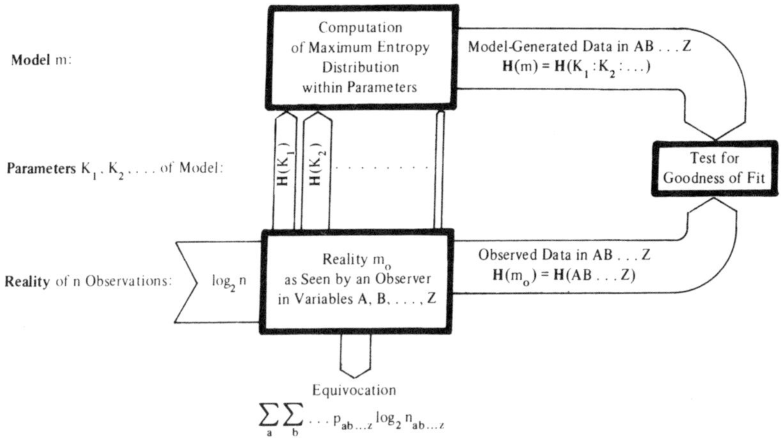

Figure 19

sent here the *logic* of such models, leaving quantitative accounts for Chapters 8 and 12.

Parameters

The parameters of a structural model are *relations within selected subsets of the variables modeled.* For example, Shannon's model of communication consists of a sequence of bivariate components, each realizing a relation in pairs of variables, ultimately linking an input to an output through a chain of components, excluding all bypasses and higher-order interactions. The choice of parameters may have technical, theoretical, empirical, or even aesthetic motivations. A technical reason for adopting certain parameters might stem from knowledge of the system modeled. If two variables are not connected in reality, an appropriate model need not consider this relation. A theoretical reason might rely on the dependencies that an existing theory anticipates. An empirical reason might point to evidence that the parameters chosen are those minimally necessary to reproduce the given data. An aesthetic reason might be based on preferences for certain kinds of explanations—simple ones, for instance.

When data are *quantitative*, parameters may be defined by mathematical functions. For example, the equation $y = r_{xy}(x) + e_y$ describes a linear relation between the two variables X and Y. Because data rarely exhibit such a one-to-one relation (function), as the coefficient r_{xy} implies, an error term e_y is added to express the deviation in Y from this ideal line and yields a closer approximation to what the data actually

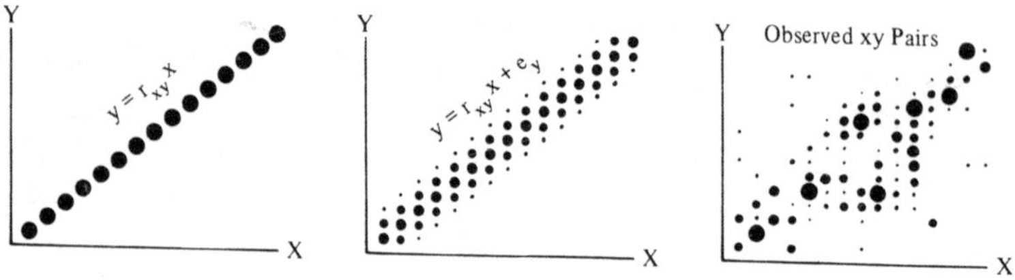

Figure 20

show. Figure 20 depicts three quantitative relations illustrating this point.

When data are *qualitative*, functional expressions such as those underlying Figure 20 are inappropriate because addition and multiplication do not apply to unordered variables. What would be appropriate here is the use of the very distribution of cooccurrences in the original data—for example, data in Figures 5, 10, and 13, the distribution of observed pairs in Figure 20, all of which constitute the most obvious and uncontaminated manifestation of relations among variables. Observed cooccurrences may not have the aesthetic appeal that mathematical equations have, but because all equations can be represented distributionally, as Figure 20 shows, the form is not only the more universal of the two but also avoids several errors.

First, functions are idealizations, many of them assuming linearity, as suggested in Figure 20. The reliance on the very distribution of observational data from which such functions could have been estimated avoids the bias inherent in mathematical simplicity.

Second, the use of variance terms, e_y in our example, assumes that deviations from the ideal conform to a standard statistical distribution, the normal distribution for example. Such an assumption is not only unnecessarily restrictive but also violates the qualitative nature of our data.

Third, the coefficients r_{xy} of structural equations, and many familiar mathematical operations (including those represented by the arrows of path diagrams), are all binary and relate pairs of variables only. Natural language also favors the expression of binary relations (opposites, contrasts, differences, causes) at the virtual exclusion of higher-order interactions. Even Shannon's original conception of communication is limited in this way. An analysis that relies on binary relations at the expense of relations of higher ordinality cannot capture the complexity that may be manifest in multivariate data.

Returning to the parameters of structural models, each relation within a designated set of variables may be said to specify a different *component* of a model. In the block diagram we shall use to depict such models, parameters are represented by boxes to which some variables are attached by lines. We say "attached" because these variables may be inputs or outputs, as in Shannon's communication chain, or simply observed variables without causal implications. The number of variables involved in a parameter equals that component's *ordinality*. The second model in Figure 21 contains one fourth-order component, ABCE, and two third-order components, BCD and CDE. Researchers familiar with path diagrams and causal networks, in which nodes represent variables and lines represent influences, must make a gestalt switch here, converting lines into boxes and nodes into lines. Block diagrams are capable of representing higher-order interactions (in boxes). Graphical devices that represent influences by arrows or dependencies by lines between variables cannot capture anything above an ordinality of two.

We can think of a component of an ordinality of one as a simple random generator that reproduces the distribution of frequencies or probabilities as originally observed in the one variable attached to it. By extension, a component of higher ordinality can be thought of as a random generator that reproduces the distribution of frequencies or probabilities of cooccurrences through which the observed relation between the attached variables is empirically manifest.

Composition

A structural model consists of several components, each specified by a different parameter with respect to which it corresponds to the data to be modeled, and *none is included or equivalent to another*. I consider here the logic for composing such models (see Klir, 1976, 1981) and define appropriate terms.

A model is said to *cover* the variables it models. Figure 21 shows four different models covering the same set of five variables. The first does not differentiate components. It represents the data in their original form by a single, all-encompassing component of ordinality five without simplification and is called the *saturated model*. We refer to this extreme case of a model by m_o. Here the saturated model is m_o = ABCDE. The second consists of three components, K_1 = ABCE, K_2 = BCD, and K_3 = CDE, and is denoted by m_i = ABCE:BCD:CDE. The third is derived from m_i by omitting the CDE component, which does not change its cover. The fourth consists of five components, one for each variable; and because they work entirely independently of each other, we denote this condition by the subscript "ind." The *model of independent variables* is m_{ind} = A:B:C:D:E.

A model's *components must be neither included nor equivalent* relative to one another and *are connected by the variables they share*. One

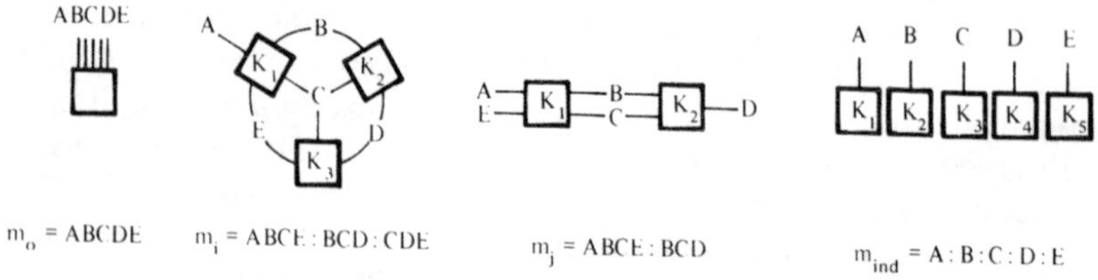

Figure 21

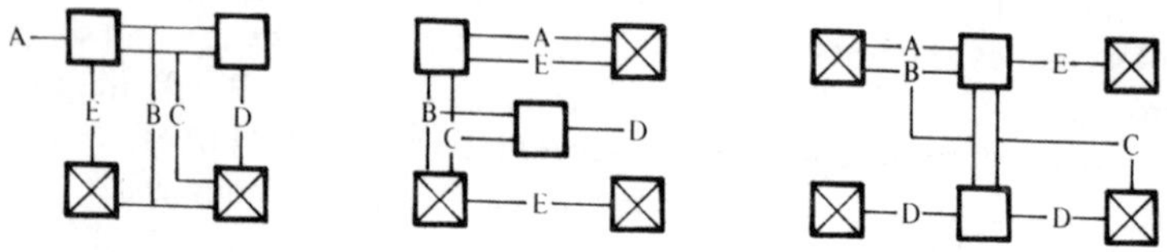

Figure 22

component is included in another if all of the former's variables are also variables of the latter. Two components are equivalent if they cover the same variables. The restriction is motivated by the fact that an explanation of a relation already explained adds nothing and is redundant. Figure 22 shows three mere graphical variates of the model m_j = ABCE:BCD of Figure 21 in which the redundant components are crossed and should be omitted.

In the model ABCE:BCD:CDE of Figure 21, variable A is said to be *unique* to the first component K_1 = ABCE because A occurs in no other component of that model. BC is *shared* between the first and the second component, and we note this fact by writing $K_1\&K_2$ = BC. Similarly, $K_1\&K_3$ = CE and $K_2\&K_3$ = CD. $K_1\&K_2\&K_3$ = C is shared among all three components. In a block diagram each variable occurs only once, regardless of how many components it connects.

The "behavioral" interpretation of the connections among the boxes of a block diagram is that components either communicate with each other or coordinate their behavior but only along the variables they share. In a chain one component's output is the next component's input, and the two components are thereby no longer independent. In the model ABCE:BCD:CDE of Figure 21, communication among components is *circular* and the loop involves variables B, D, and E. Block diagrams are much like the process diagrams in management or like the wiring diagrams in electrical engineering in which lines indicate connections among components or what is transmitted between them.

Interactions

A parameter—that is, a probability distribution within a subset of the variables covered by a model—contains all complexities that a component can represent, particularly all relations of an ordinality less than the number of variables involved. Thus the parameter ABCD contains four tertiary relations—ABC, ABD, ACD, and BCD—six binary relations—AB, AC, AD, BC, BD, and CD—four unary relations in separate variables—A, B, C, and D—and the nominal ϕ. The parameter ABC

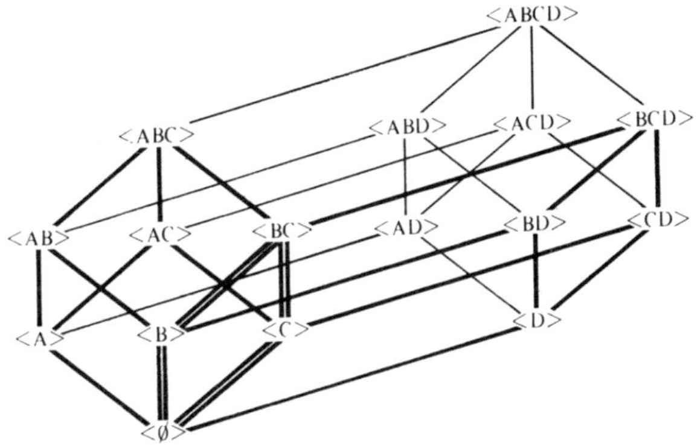

Figure 23

contains AB, AC, BC, A, B, C, and ϕ, all of which are already contained in ABCD. This embeddedness motivates the demand that the components of a model are neither included nor equivalent relative to each other and led to calling such models *hierarchical.*

However, there arises the need to consider what is unique to a set of variables—for example, what is unique to ABC and not reducible to AB, AC, BC, or to what any of these contain. This is called an *interaction.* An interaction is *a unique dependency from which all relations of a lower ordinality are removed.* All of its variables are essential; none can be omitted. By this definition interactions are not embedded in each other, can be said to be the additive content of a relation, and form Boolean lattices. We use "<" and ">" to distinguish interactions from the parameters that contain them. Figure 23 depicts the interactional content of the relation ABCD.

Except for the satured model, m_o, which contains all interactions possible within the original data, *all other models exclude some interactions.* Figure 23 also depicts the interactions contained in the model ABC:BCD, using heavy lines to connect them. Interactions excluded from this model are connected by fine lines, and interactions shared by the two components are connected by two heavy lines. As indicated in this figure, in lattices of all possible interactions, relations form sublattices, one for each component and one for each shared set of variables.

Relations Between Models: Descendency

Two models are said to have the *same structure* or are of the same *structure type* if one can be obtained from the other by a mere one-to-one relabeling of its variables. For example, the models ABCE:BCD:CDE (see Figure 21) and ABCE:ABD:ADE have the same structure because the latter can be obtained from the former by exchanging A with C in all components. Models of the same structure yield the same block diagrams except for the labels on their connecting lines. Block diagrams without labels depict structure types (see Figure 25).

Structural modeling often requires comparisons of models. For this purpose we define the notion of *descendency*. One model is said to be a descendent of another *if all relations in the former model are included in the latter* and both models cover the same variables. Descendent models are also called *nested* models. For example, the model AB:AD:BCDE is a descendent of ABD:BCDE because AB and AD are included in ABD and BCDE occurs in both. Two models of which neither is a descendent of the other are *incompatible*. For example, the model AC:BCDE, which contains AC, is incompatible with ABD:BCDE and AB:AD:BCDE because AC is absent from both. We denote descendency by an *arrow from an ancestor to its descendent*: for example, ABD:BCDE→AB:AD:BCDE, or more generally $m_i \rightarrow m_j$.

A model is a direct or *immediate descendent* of another if no intermediate models exist and the two models *differ by only one interaction.* For example, the following string denotes one of several possible lines of immediate descendents of ABD:BCDE:

$$\text{ABD : BCDE} \rightarrow \text{AB : AD : BCDE} \rightarrow \text{AB : BCDE} \rightarrow \text{A : BCDE}$$

$$\rightarrow \text{A : BCD : BCE : BDE : CDE}$$

Here interactions <ABD>, <AD>, <AB> and <BCDE> are removed in this order, reaching A:BCD:BCE:BDE:CDE in four steps. Klir (1976) calls these steps "immediate refinements" as they introduce simpler components. An algorithm for generating a model's immediate descendents is given in Chapter 14. Given that an ancestor always represents greater complexity than any of its descendents, the number of immediate descendents that separate two models can serve as a measure of the difference in their complexity. Figure 24 includes this number.

Lattices

Models that cover the same variables always have one nearest common ancestor and one nearest common descendent. The *nearest common*

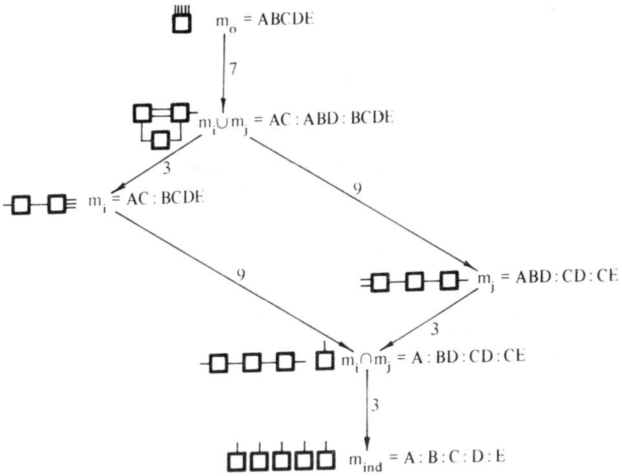

Figure 24

ancestor is composed of all and only the *components* of the models being compared, except those included or equivalent relative to each other. For example, when putting the two incompatible models AC:BCDE and ABD:CD:CE together, CD and CE of the second model are contained in BCDE of the first and are redundant in any common ancestor. The remaining components, AC:ABD:BCDE, constitute the nearest common ancestor of the two models. The *nearest common descendent* contains all and only the *interactions* shared by the models being compared. Using the same two models as an example, ABD:CD:CE contains<ABD>, <AB>, <AD>, <BD>, <CD>, and <CE>, of which only the last three are shared with AC:BCDE. Given that none of the interactions involving A is shared, the nearest common descendent will include A as a separate variable and BC, CD, and CE as components. The resulting A:BD:CD:CE, retains all shared interactions, preserves the distinctions made by either model, and is their nearest common descendent.

As already mentioned, generic references to models are helpful, m_i or m_j referring to a model in general, or $K_1:K_2:\ldots:K_r$ referring to a model's r components. The nearest common ancestor of two models is denoted by "$m_i \cup m_j$" and the nearest common descent by $m_i \cap m_j$. The saturated model, m_o, representing the data without simplification, can be called the *most distant common ancestor*, and m_{ind}, the least complex of all possible models, can be called the *most distant common descendent*. It follows that for any two models, covering the same variables

$$m_o \rightarrow m_i \cup m_j \rightarrow m_i \rightarrow m_i \cap m_j \rightarrow m_{ind} \qquad [6.1]$$

$$m_o \rightarrow m_i \cup m_j \rightarrow m_j \rightarrow m_i \cap m_j \rightarrow m_{ind}$$

These relationships define a lattice, which is depicted in Figure 24 using the above models as an example. The numbers indicate how many generations these models are apart.

Lattices of structural models as in Figure 24 differ from the Boolean lattices of all possible interactions as in Figure 23. Lattices of all possible models provide important guides for analysts of qualitative data to find their way through the forest of models to be considered. They also form

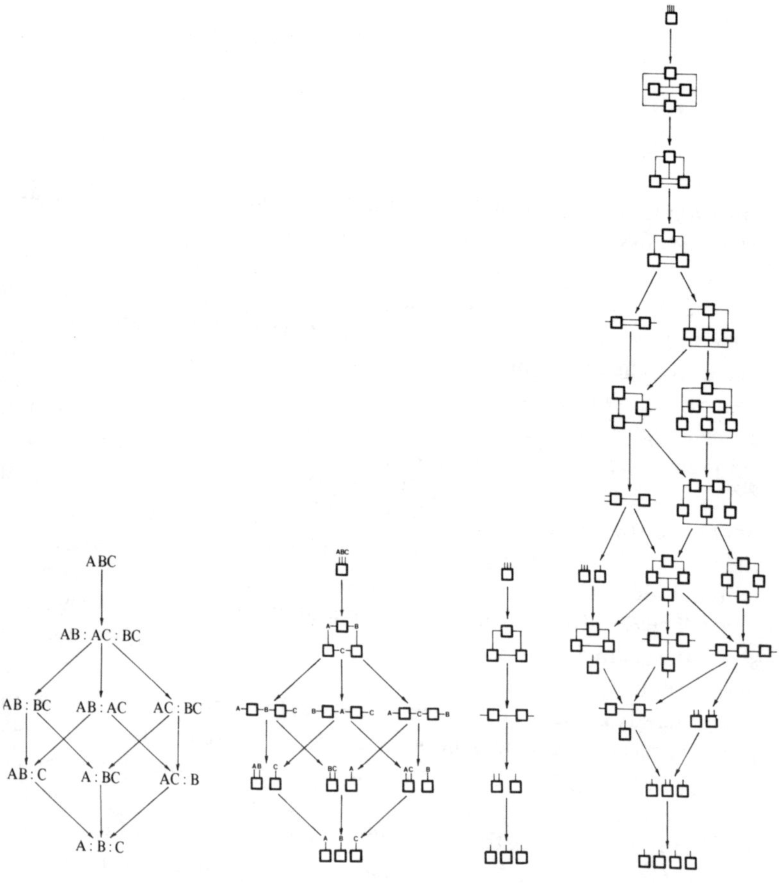

Figure 25

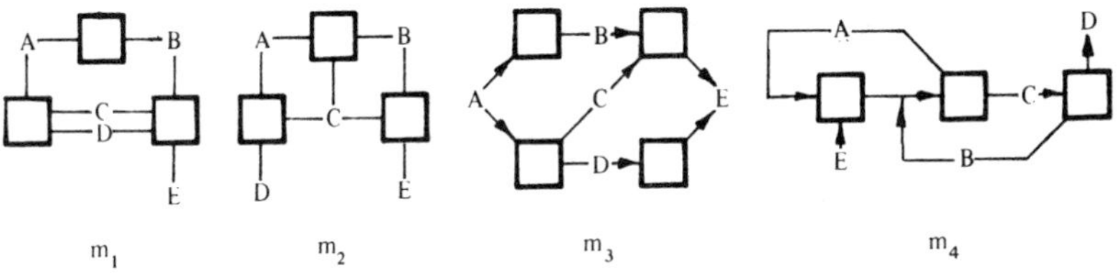

Figure 26

the basis of computer programs for exploratory analysis. To appreciate the kind of lattices we have to be concerned with, Figure 25 depicts two versions of the lattice of all models in three variables and two lattices of all structure types of models in three and four variables, respectively. Chapter 14 considers algorithms for the generation of such lattices.

7. MODELS WITH AND WITHOUT LOOPS

Shannon's communication chain is the prototype of a structural model without loops. The output of one component is the input to the next. There is no feedback. Causality goes one way only. No component influences itself, directly or indirectly. Models without loops can be evaluated sequentially, and convenient algebraic (so-called closed form) expressions for computing the maximum entropy probabilities are made available in Chapters 12 and 14. For structural models with loops, algebraic expressions are unavailable and maximum entropy probabilities must be computed iteratively (see Chapter 12), requiring electronic computers. This difference motivates the distinction elaborated in this chapter.

When models are simple, loops are easily recognizable by their circularity. But when models cover many variables and dependencies among them are complex, a visual inspection of block diagrams may be misleading. Consider the examples in Figure 26. Here m_1 clearly contains a loop involving A-B-CD and back to A, but the structure in the others might not be so transparent.

To detect whether a structural model contains loops, we use an algorithm similar to the one suggested by Bishop, Fienberg, and Holland (1978:76):

Given the components $K_1, K_2, \ldots, K_e, K_f, \ldots$ of a model

(1) remove all variables that are unique to any K_e

(2) remove any K_e that is equal to or contained in any other K_f of the (remaining) set.

Repeat 1 and 2 until either

(a) no variables remain, in which case loops are absent, or

(b) the remainder is unalterable by 1 or 2, in which case loops exist.

Take m_2 of Figure 26 for the first example:

Given: ABC:ACD:BCE
by 1: ABC:AC:BC
by 2: ABC
by 1: ϕ
Hence m_2 does not contain loops.

Applied to m_3 of Figure 26:

Given: AB:ACD:BCE:DE
by 1: AB:ACD:BCE:DE (no unique variable)
by 2: AB:ACD:BCE:DE (no K equal to or contained in another)
Hence m_3 does contain loops, namely A-B-E-D-A, A-B-C-A and C-D-E-C

Applied to m_4 of Figure 26:

Given: ABC:ABE:BCD
by 1: ABC:AB:BC
by 2: ABC
by 1: ϕ
Hence m_4 does not contain loops.

Actually, m_2 and m_4 have the same structure (one can be obtained from the other by exchanging labels), and the test is redundant. Their different appearances demonstrate that block diagrams can hide the existence of loops or falsely suggest them. The formal test is conclusive, however.

Note that the direction of causality does not enter the test for whether a model contains loops. For example, m_3 = AB:ACD:BCE:DE cannot be altered by our algorithm and is therefore said to contain loops; even so, the causality indicated by the arrows in Figure 26 is unidirectional. Also the distinction between *nonrecursive* and *recursive* models, which is made in the literature on modeling quantitative data, does not always coincide with the distinction between models with and without loops. Because of the absence of circular causalities, m_3 would be considered a recursive model even though it does contain loops.

This algorithm is merely intended to separate structures according to their unequal computational requirements. However, the sequence leading to the determination that loops are absent is nothing but the inverse of a recursive procedure by which such models could be constructed by extending components to cover additional variables or by adding components with new variables to an existing model. The probabilities generated by loopless models are computable in the same order. Test results leading to the conclusion that loops exist point to a set of variables within which some loop(s) make sequential computations impossible, requiring iterative processes instead.

8. INFORMATION IN MODELS AND IN DATA

We stated that structural models that reproduce given data reasonably well can serve as an explanation of those data. To assess their goodness of fit, measures are now needed that compare the artificial data generated by a model with the original data. In this chapter we will extend Shannon's initially bivariate notion of information and develop the instrumentarium needed to quantify how much of the information present in data is represented in a particular model or ignored by it. These information quantities not only provide criteria for deciding how good a model is but will also guide the exploration of alternative model structures.

To begin with McGill (1954) and Ashby's (1969) generalization of Shannon and Weaver's (1949) notion of information, we observe that 4.12 is in fact composed of two separate entropies, the entropy in model m_{ind}= A:B:C:...:Z, whose variables are all independent, and the entropy in the saturated model m_o = ABC...Z, both covering the same variables:

$$\begin{aligned} \mathbf{T}(A:B:C:\ldots:Z) & \\ &= \mathbf{H}(A)+\mathbf{H}(B)+\mathbf{H}(C)+\ldots+\mathbf{H}(Z)-\mathbf{H}(ABC\ldots Z) \\ &= \mathbf{H}(A:B:C:\ldots:Z) - \mathbf{H}(ABC\ldots Z) \\ &= \mathbf{H}(m_{ind}) - \mathbf{H}(m_o) \\ &= \mathbf{T}(m_{ind}) \end{aligned} \quad [8.1]$$

$\mathbf{H}(m_o)$ conforms to 3.5 and is the entropy in the original data that contain all complexities a model might hope to explain within the variables covered. It is also the smallest entropy a model of these data can generate. $\mathbf{H}(m_{ind})$ is the entropy in a model of independent variables that excludes all relations among variables the data could contain. Being computed as the sum of the entropies in the individual variables, by 4.1, it is also the maximum entropy obtainable within the given set of variables and the entropy of the so-called maximum likelihood distribution to which only the knowledge of the distribution in individual variables enters (Gokhale and Kullback, 1978). The difference between the two, the total amount of information, $\mathbf{T}(m_{ind})$, *is the maximum amount of information in the data that a model can conceivably explain.* $\mathbf{T}(A:B)$ in 4.4 through 4.7 is its simplest form.

In developing the required information quantities, we proceed in two steps. The first is to generalize $\mathbf{T}(m_{ind})$ in 8.1 to more complex models. Let $p_{ab\ldots z}$ be the probabilities in the data (or "generated" by m_o) and let $\rho_{abc\ldots z}$ be the probabilities generated by a model m_j. Then, by analogy to 4.7,

$$\mathbf{T}(m_j) = \sum_a \sum_b \cdots \sum_z p_{abc..z} \log_2 \frac{p_{abc..z}}{\rho_{abc..z}} \qquad [8.2]$$

$\mathbf{T}(m_o) = 0$ and for models m_j with loops:

$$\mathbf{T}(m_j) \neq \mathbf{H}(m_j) - \mathbf{H}(m_o) \qquad [8.3]$$

Given that $\mathbf{T}(m_{ind})$ is the amount of information m_o can and m_{ind} cannot explain, $\mathbf{T}(m_j)$ must be interpreted as *the amount of information in the data* m_o *that escapes an account by model* m_j. It measures by how much m_j is in error and indicates the quantity that structural modeling efforts aim to minimize.

The second step toward the desired generalization concerns information measures that permit comparisons *between descendent models.* Let there be two such models, m_i and m_j of which m_i generates distributions of probabilities $\omega_{abc\ldots z}$ and m_j generates distributions of probabilities $\rho_{abc\ldots z}$. The *informational difference*—that is, the amount of information modeled in m_i but ignored in m_j—is

$$\mathbf{I}(m_i \rightarrow m_j) = \sum_a \sum_b \cdots \sum_z p_{abc..z} \log_2 \frac{\omega_{abc..z}}{\rho_{abc..z}} \qquad [8.4]$$

This most general definition of information lends itself to what is probably the most important *identity for partitioning* quantities of information. It is attributed to Gokhale and Kullback (1978):

$$\mathbf{I}(m_o \rightarrow m_{ind}) = \mathbf{I}(m_o \rightarrow m_j) + \mathbf{I}(m_j \rightarrow m_{ind}) \qquad [8.5]$$

This definition decomposes the total amount of information in the data, $\mathbf{I}(m_o \rightarrow m_{ind})$, into one quantity, $\mathbf{I}(m_j \rightarrow m_{ind})$, for which the model m_j accounts, and another quantity, $\mathbf{I}(m_o \rightarrow m_j)$, by which that model is in error, the latter being due to the differences between the observed and the model-generated data.

For a line of descendent models, 8.5 is extendable to any number of models whose informational differences are related as follows:

$$\mathbf{I}(m_o \rightarrow m_{ind}) = \mathbf{I}(m_o \rightarrow m_i) + \mathbf{I}(m_i \rightarrow m_j) + \mathbf{I}(m_j \rightarrow m_{ind}) \qquad [8.6]$$

This accounting equation enables the analyst to assess not only how much information a given model ignores and represents in its structure, respectively, but also by how much another model would improve its "fit." We shall use both forms, 8.5 primarily for confirmation and 8.6 primarily for exploration. For algebraic convenience, the informational difference in 8.4 may also be stated in **T**-terms:

$$\mathbf{I}(m_i \rightarrow m_j) = \mathbf{I}(m_o \rightarrow m_j) - \mathbf{I}(m_o \rightarrow m_i) = \mathbf{T}(m_j) - \mathbf{T}(m_i) \qquad [8.7]$$

Figure 27 relates the quantities in 8.5 through 8.7 graphically within a stylized lattice of all possible models with the same cover.

For an algebraic example of the two information quantities, **I** and **T**, take *Shannon's chain*, AB:BC:CD:...:YZ. Considering 8.5 and 8.7, and taking full advantage of the algebraic properties of the information quantities associated with loopless models, we find the following equivalence:

$$\mathbf{I}(m_o \rightarrow m_{ind}) \quad = \quad \mathbf{I}(m_o \rightarrow m_{chain}) \quad + \mathbf{I}(m_{chain} \rightarrow m_{ind}) \qquad [8.8]$$

$$\mathbf{T}(A:B:C:\ldots:Z) = \mathbf{T}(AB:BC:CD:\ldots:YZ)$$

$$+ \mathbf{T}(A:B) + \mathbf{T}(B:C) + \mathbf{T}(C:D) + \ldots + \mathbf{T}(Y:Z)$$

Whereas the sum **T**(A:B) + **T**(B:C) + ... + **T**(Y:Z) expresses the information transmitted within the chain, the quantity **T**(AB:BC:...:YZ) summarizes all quantities of information transmitted between nonsuccessive pairs of variables—for example, **T**(A:C), **T**(A:Z), **T**(B:Z)—and contained in higher-order interactions which the chain cannot represent. If the reality the data represents is indeed chainlike, then the latter and, for this chain, extraneous quantities will be zero and the total amount of information equals the sum of the transmissions within components as in 4.13. If these extraneous quantities are non-zero, then these error quantities suggest that the reality of the data is not quite as chainlike as the model supposes. Equation 8.8 also demonstrates that the informational differences between models, expressed in **I**-measures,

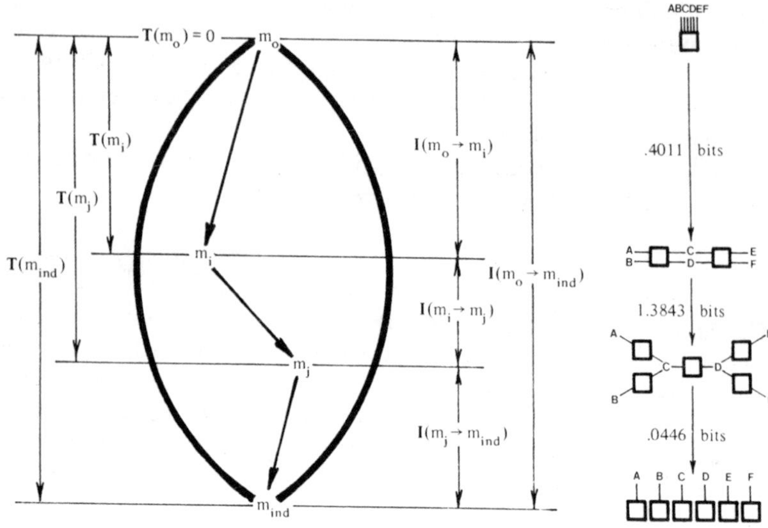

Figure 27

implicitly represent quantities of information transmitted between variables, expressed in **T**-measures, whereby the latter need not have the same covers.

For a numerical example, consider 18 hypothetical observations in six binary variables A through F of two values, 0 or 1 each, as listed in Figure 28. The total amount of information in these data is 1.8301 bits. Of this, the model ABCD:CDEF accounts for 1.4290 bits, or 78%, and fails to account for the remaining .4011 bits. These quantities are found in Figure 27 as well. The model AC:BC:CD:DE:DF accounts for only .0446 bits, or 2% of the total amount, and fails to account for 1.7854 bits. Clearly in this instance, the simpler model is totally inadequate. It ignores the information accounted for by higher-order interactions present in the data. This finding would lead to the conclusion that a theory that might be used to explain these data cannot be constructed in terms of the binary relations in AC:BC:CD:DE:DF. A more appropriate theory should state at least two fourth-order relationships between variables and, if it does just this, can then explain no more than 78% of the information that could be accounted for.

A:	0	0	0	0	0	0	0	0	0	1	1	1	1	1	1	1	1	1
B:	0	0	0	0	1	1	1	1	1	0	0	0	0	0	1	1	1	1
C:	0	0	1	1	0	0	1	1	1	0	0	0	1	1	0	0	1	1
D:	0	0	1	1	1	1	0	0	1	0	1	1	0	0	0	0	1	1
E:	0	1	0	1	0	1	0	1	0	1	0	1	0	1	0	1	0	1
F:	0	1	0	1	1	0	1	0	1	0	1	0	1	0	0	1	0	1

Figure 28

We shall later require an expression of the maximum value of the quantity $\mathbf{I}(m_i \rightarrow m_j)$. Without justification, this maximum is

$$\mathbf{I}(m_i \rightarrow m_j)_{max} = \mathbf{I}(m_i \rightarrow m_j) + \sum_{K \in m_i} \{H(K) - \max_{L \in m_j} [\mathbf{H}(K \& L)]\} \quad [8.9]$$

where K is a component of m_i, L is a component of m_j, and K&L consists of the variables shared by the two components K and L.

Note that all information quantities so far considered pertain to *models as a whole.* They differentiate neither the contributions made by its component parts (the expression in **T**-terms for the chain is an exception) nor the contributions made by particular interactions. We shall address some of these issues in Chapter 14. Note also that we have not yet stated how the probabilities generated by these models are computed and compared with available data; Chapter 12 concerns this issue. Finally, the problem of testing the significance of the information quantities will be addressed in Chapters 10 and 11.

9. STRUCTURAL ZEROS

In multivariate spaces some cells may remain empty or have zero observed frequencies. Three reasons could account for such cells, the last being our primary concern. The first is empirical. Zero frequencies may be due to existing constraints in the data source, and evidence of this nature may contribute to the research findings. Second, zero frequencies may be due to sample sizes that are too small to contain all possible observations. Sampling theory contends that with increasing sample sizes each possible observation will eventually occur at least once, no matter how rare the case may be. Significance tests aim at differentiating between the two kinds of reasons. The third reason is logical or theoretical. Frequencies may be zero because observations are impossible or excluded on a priori grounds. Such cells are different from the other two in that expected probabilities are zero as well. A zero frequency therefore may have quite different interpretations.

A zero in a cell for empirically possible observations (for which expected probabilities are non-zero) is called an *observational zero*, whereas a zero in an unoccupiable cell or in a cell for which observations are impossible (and expected probabilities are zero as well) is called a *structural zero.*

For example, consider data on "who follows whom" in a study of turn taking during a group discussion. Given that no person can take the turn to speak away from himself or herself, all diagonal cells of the square

To Whom:

Who:	1	2	3	4
1	–	n_{12}	n_{13}	n_{14}
2	n_{21}	–	n_{23}	n_{24}
3	n_{31}	n_{32}	–	n_{34}
4	n_{41}	n_{42}	n_{43}	–

Higher Rank:

Lower Rank:	1	2	3	4	5
1	–	n_{12}	n_{13}	n_{14}	n_{15}
2	–	–	n_{23}	n_{24}	n_{25}
3	–	–	–	n_{34}	n_{35}
4	–	–	–	–	n_{45}

Figure 29

matrix in Figure 29 will contain structural zeros. A model generating expected probabilities with which observed frequencies are to be compared must not enter anything in these unoccupiable cells either. Or consider the cross-tabulation of messages exchanged between individuals of higher and lower ranks within a corporation that recognizes five levels of employment. Given that "higher rank" and "lower rank" are defined in terms of the difference in rank, only a triangle of the matrix in Figure 29 is occupiable. The remaining cells contain structural zeros. Structural zeros do not need to be distributed as regularly as in Figure 29. Further examples are found in Figure 32.

Structural zeros *destroy the strict Cartesian orthogonality of complete multivariate spaces* that are formed by the simple product of their variables, and complicate computations by structural models (specifically the generation of maximum entropy probability distributions and the evaluation of their degrees of freedom). In contrast, observational zeros do not contribute to the information measures and require no special considerations.

10. DEGREES OF FREEDOM

Degrees of freedom enumerate the non-zero probabilities that a model needs to compute (estimate) within its parameters. This number is required for testing the significance of the information quantities.

The most elementary constraint on the choice of probabilities is that their sum must equal unity or, with reference to frequencies, their sum must equal the known sample size. Accordingly, and with N categories or cells, we can estimate only N − 1 probabilities, after which the probability in the Nth cell is no longer a matter of choice. Thus within a variable or space K, the *degree of freedom* (**df**) for simple entropies **H**(K) is

$$\mathbf{df}_K = N_K - 1 \qquad [10.1]$$

Structural models impose the additional constraint that the computed probabilities must conform to that model's parameters. In the 3×5 matrix AB of Figure 30, for example, there are $\mathbf{df}_{AB} = N_{AB} - 1 = 15 - 1 = 14$ degrees of freedom. The parameters of the model A:B with its two independent components (variables) A and B have $\mathbf{df}_A = N_A - 1 = 3 - 1 = 2$ and $\mathbf{df}_B = N_B - 1 = 5 - 1 = 4$ degrees of freedom, respectively, and $\mathbf{df}_{A:B} = \mathbf{df}_A + \mathbf{df}_B = 2 + 4 = 6$ in total.

The removal of one ineraction <ABC...> from a model *without structural zeros* removes

$$\mathbf{df}_{ABC...} - \mathbf{df}_{\overline{<ABC...>}} = (N_A - 1)(N_B - 1)(N_C - 1)... \qquad [10.2]$$

degrees of freedom. In the example $\mathbf{df}_{AB} - \mathbf{df}_{A:B} = (3-1)(5-1) = 8$.

For models that have *neither loops nor structural zeros,* 10.2 generalizes this notion to models $m = K_1:...: K_e:K_f:...:$

$$\mathbf{df}_m = \sum_e \mathbf{df}_{K_e} \qquad [10.3]$$

$$- \sum_e \sum_{f>e} \mathbf{df}_{K_e \& K_f}$$

$$+ \sum_e \sum_{f>e} \sum_{g>f} \mathbf{df}_{K_e \& K_f \& K_g}$$

− degrees of freedom in sets of variables shared among four components

+ etc.

For testing the significance of information quantities $\mathbf{I}(m_i \rightarrow m_j)$, involving two descendent models without structural zeros, the degree of freedom is

$$\mathbf{df}_{m_i \rightarrow m_j} = \mathbf{df}_{m_i} - \mathbf{df}_{m_j} \qquad [10.4]$$

In Figure 30, $\mathbf{df}_{AB \rightarrow A:B} = \mathbf{df}_{AB} - \mathbf{df}_{A:B} = 14 - 6 = 8$ degrees of freedom. The matrix labeled AB→A:B illustrates this condition. Because each model must satisfy its parameters, this maximum entropy distribution must satisfy the requirement that rows and columns add to the marginal probabilities in A and in B. Of the $3 \times 5 = 15$ cells, the seven shaded cells are implied or fixed once the eight unshaded cells are chosen, hence $\mathbf{df}_{AB \to A:B} = 8$ as obtained above. For the five structure types possible

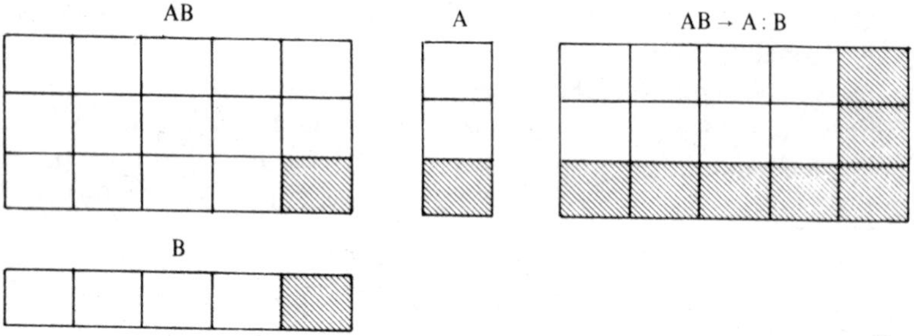

Figure 30

within three variables (see Figure 25), the degrees of freedom are listed in Figure 31. The entries in this table take advantage of the fact that in the absence of structural zeros, multivariate spaces are Cartesian products of its variables—that is, $N_{ABC...} = N_A N_B N_C \ldots$. Because each model in this table is an immediate descendent of the one above, the column lists the degrees of freedom for the interactions eliminated during this descent. The individual degrees of freedom sum to the total $\mathbf{df}_{m_o \to m_{ind}}$. The table should be familiar to χ^2 users.

i	m_i	$\mathbf{df}_{m_i}$	Interaction Removed $m_i \to m_{i+1}$	$\mathbf{df}_{m_i \to m_{i+1}}$
0	ABC	$N_{ABC} - 1$	<ABC>	$(N_A-1)(N_B-1)(N_C-1)$
1	AB : AC : BC	$N_{AB} + N_{AC} + N_{BC} - N_A - N_B - N_C$	<BC>	$(N_B-1)(N_C-1)$
2	AB : AC	$N_{AB} + N_{AC} - N_A - 1$	<AC>	$(N_A-1)(N_C-1)$
3	AB : C	$N_{AB} + N_C - 2$	<AB>	$(N_A-1)(N_B-1)$
4	A : B : C	$N_A + N_B + N_C - 3$		
				$N_{ABC} - N_A - N_B - N_C + 2$

Figure 31

For *models with structural zeros*, degrees of freedom cannot be determined by unqualified multiplication. Cells with structural zeros or with unalterably fixed probabilities must be discounted not only numerically but also regarding their positions relative to each other. We propose the following three-step procedure:

(1) (a) Start with the original space ABC...Z, covering the same variables as the model $m = K_1:K_2:...$

(b) Assign zeros to all cells of ABC...Z with structural zeros and with a priori and fixed probabilities (neither of which is estimated) and assign ones to all other cells.

(c) Obtain cell entries for each of m's parameters K by summing over the corresponding cell entries (zero or one) in ABC...Z.

(d) Change to zero the entries in those cells of ABC...Z that participate in yielding the sum of unity in any cell of a parameter K.

(e) Repeat c and d until the distribution of zeros and ones remains unchanged.

(f) Determine whether the cells in ABC...Z with ones are separable into parts R of ABC...Z. Two submatrices or subspaces of a multivariate space are separable if they have no categories or qualities in common.

(g) For each part R separately, sum its entries to cells in each component K. Call the set of cells with non-zero entries in K: K_R.

(2) Compute the degrees of freedom according to 10.1 through 10.4 but separately for each part R and its corresponding K_Rs. The degree of freedom $\mathbf{df}_{m_0 \rightarrow m}$ is the sum of the degrees of freedom obtained for each of its parts.

(3) Given the above results for any pair of models, of which *one must be a descendent of the other*, compute the difference in the degrees of freedom by

$$\mathbf{df}_{m_i \rightarrow m_j} = \mathbf{df}_{m_o \rightarrow m_j} - \mathbf{df}_{m_o \rightarrow m_i} \qquad [10.5]$$

In essence, step 1 removes so-called noninteractive cells, whose probabilities are not free to be estimated, and it distinguishes among submatrices or subspaces whose degrees of freedom must be considered separately. Step 2 computes the degree of freedom $\mathbf{df}_{m_0 \rightarrow m}$ used in step 3 to obtain $\mathbf{df}_{m_i \rightarrow m_j}$. Equation 10.5 is the general form of 10.4. We illustrate the process with the four examples from Figure 32.

Suppose the null hypothesis A:B of the independence of A and B is to be tested with structural zeros distributed as in the first of the three matrices in Figure 32. Step 1b assigns zeros to the nine cells with structural zeros and ones to the seven occupiable cells. Summing these entries toward the margins, step 1c yields ones in cell 4 of A and in cell 1 of B. Step 1d then changes to zero the cells 11 and 44 of AB which are responsible for the ones in A and in B. Step 1c then finds ones in 1 of A and 4 of B, causing step 1d to change 12 and 34 of AB to zero, and so on

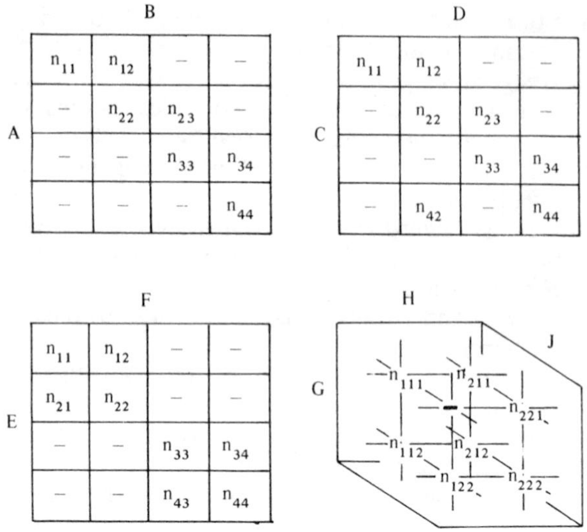

Figure 32

until, as it turns out in this case, all cells are zero. As there obviously is a sequence for computing all probabilities in AB from those in A and B, which this procedure actually traces, there are no options, no degrees of freedom, and there is in fact no information in the data that the model does not already contain in its parameters. The set of values to be estimated being empty, the degrees of freedom is zero.

Suppose the null hypothesis C:D is to be tested with structural zeros as distributed in the second matrix of Figure 32. Here step 1c finds a one in cell 1 of D causing step 1d to change cell 11 of CD to zero, then step 1c finds a one in cell 1 of C, causing step 1d to change cell 12 of CD to zero. At this point the iteration stops. The remaining six ones remain in place. Because the matrix is not separable, we compute the degrees of freedom from this remaining set as a whole. According to step 2, we find $\mathbf{df}_{CD} = 6 - 1 = 5$, $\mathbf{df}_C = \mathbf{df}_D = 3 - 1 = 2$, $\mathbf{df}_{CD \to C:D} = 5 - 2 - 2 = 1$, and, indeed, only one of the six probabilities in this matrix needs to be estimated for all the other probabilities to become known.

When the third of these matrices is subjected to the same test, the configuration of zeros and ones assigned by step 1b remains unalterable by 1c and by 1d. However, the matrix is clearly separable into two 2×2 submatrices. To obtain the degrees of freedom for the whole matrix, we take the two separable parts individually. Each 2×2 matrix contributes one degree of freedom, which brings the degree of freedom $\mathbf{df}_{EF \to E:F}$ in the matrix as a whole to two.

In the last example of Figure 32 the cube of 2 × 2 × 2 cells has only one structural zero. Several models can be applied in this case. Under the model G:H:J, none of the seven possible cells is removable by step 1, nothing is separable, hence R consists of the seven cells. Then according to step 2, $\mathbf{df}_{GHJ} = 7 - 1 = 6$, $\mathbf{df}_G = \mathbf{df}_H = \mathbf{df}_J = 2 - 1 = 1$, and $\mathbf{df}_{GHJ \to G:H:J} = 7 - 1 - 1 - 1 = 4$. For the model GH: J we find only one cell, cell 111, to equal one of GH's values, the other six remain unaltered by step 1. Step 2 yields $\mathbf{df}_{GHJ} = 6 - 1 = 5$, $\mathbf{df}_{GH} = 3 - 1 = 2$, $\mathbf{df}_H = 2 - 1 = 1$, and $\mathbf{df}_{GHJ \to GH:J} = 5 - 2 - 1 = 2$. Applying step 3, $\mathbf{df}_{GH:J \to G:H:J} = 4 - 2 = 2$. For the model GH:GJ:HJ, starting with GH, cell 111 is removed as before. Combined with GJ, cells 211 and 221 are removed, leaving the remaining four cells to be uniquely determinable by values in HJ, hence $\mathbf{df}_{GHJ \to GH:GJ:HJ} = 0$. This suggests that the one structural zero here excludes third-order interactions from the data.

Alternative procedures are described by Bishop et al. (1978:115ff).

11. THE SIGNIFICANCE OF INFORMATION QUANTITIES

All information quantities express differences between two distributions of frequencies or probabilities. When the sample size of these distributions is small, sampling biases may add to these differences. It follows that information quantities obtained from a sample tend to overestimate the true information quantities in a population from which that sample was drawn and are rarely exactly zero even when there is no statistical difference between the two distributions. This led Miller (1955) to propose correction formulas that need not concern us here. What we need to decide is whether an information quantity as measured exceeds the sampling error that the sample size leads us to expect.

Miller and Meadow (1954) have shown that quantities of information and the familiar χ^2 (chi-square) values are similar in distribution. The *maximum likelihood estimate* $\mathbf{L}^2$

$$\mathbf{L}^2 = 2n \sum p \log_e \frac{p}{\pi} = 1.3863\, n\, \mathbf{I} \qquad [11.1]$$

approximates χ^2 asymptotically, and the approximation becomes the better the smaller the information quantities are. Thus with the help of the $\mathbf{L}^2$ values and the appropriate degrees of freedom, the probability (significance level) that the information quantities reflect sampling biases rather than true differences can be obtained using standard χ^2 tables.

For example, in Chapter 4 and for data in Figure 13, we found the amount of information retained between two interviews to be **T**(A:B) = 1.054 bits. The degrees of freedom in this 4 × 4 table is $\mathbf{df}_{AB \rightarrow A:B} = 9$. And with n = 266, $\mathbf{L}^2$ becomes 388.67. According to any χ^2 table, for 9 degrees of freedom we require a χ^2 of at least 27.88 in order to reject the null hypothesis at the .001 level of significance. Given that $\mathbf{L}^2$ here exceeds the required χ^2 value, the information quantity is statistically significant at this level. Or consider the data on racial biases in Figure 16 as analyzed in Figure 18. For the third school, **T**(3:B) = .187 bits, $\mathbf{df}_B = 3$, n = 272, $\mathbf{L}^2 = 70.51$ exceeds the $\chi^2 = 16.7$ required to reject the null hypothesis at the .001 level of significance. Thus there is little doubt that racial considerations matter in this school. For the fourth school, **T**(4:B) = .00013 bits, $\mathbf{df}_B = 3$, n = 140, $\mathbf{L}^2 = .03$ does not come near the χ^2 of any reasonable level of significance. Hence bias cannot be alleged here.

Note that χ^2 tests are limited to distributions whose average cell frequency is at least five, $n > 5N$. Although the violation of this restriction biases the information quantities as well, as the emphasis in this test is on the null hypothesis (of no true differences between two frequency distributions), an overestimation of information quantities feeds the Type I error of rejecting the null hypothesis when it should be accepted. However, because of the particular organization of structural models (see lattices in Figures 24 and 25), the models that do survive this test tend to be more complex than actually needed and are likely to include the true model (which would have been found had more data been available) as one of its descendents. Unlike the χ^2 test, in the context of this modeling approach, inadequate samples render the $\mathbf{L}^2$ test not inappropriate but merely more conservative. The $\mathbf{L}^2$ tests says little about the complementary error of accepting positive quantities of information as true quantities when they might be affected by inadequate sample sizes. For further comparisons see Chapter 15.

For really small sample sizes (relative to the number of cells available in a multivariate space) we refer to "bootstrap techniques" outlined by Diaconis and Efron (1983), which provide reasonable estimates of the reliabilities of the models inferred from data.

12. MAXIMUM ENTROPY COMPUTATIONS

Structural models compute a probability distribution that satisfies their parameters and is otherwise maximum in entropy. For models without loops and without structural zeros, all relevant entropies can be obtained algebraically from the entropies in a model's parameters without the need explicitly to generate maximum entropy probability distributions. The latter is required for models with loops and for many cases in which structural zeros are present. We will start with the former and then proceed to the general case.

Models Without Loops and Without Structural Zeros

The computational shortcuts available for loopless models are rooted in the fact that the probabilities such models generate are simple products of the probabilities in a model's parameters whose conditionality reflects the way components are connected. For example, the maximum entropy probabilities in the model of independent variables, A:B:C:...:Z are

$$\pi_{abc..z} = p_a \, p_b \, p_c \cdots p_z$$

In the chain AB:BC:...:YZ, similar to Figure 9, they are

$$\omega_{abc..z} = p_{ab} \, p_{c|b} \, p_{d|c} \cdots p_{z|y} = \frac{p_{ab} \, p_{bc} \, p_{cd} \cdots p_{yz}}{p_b \, p_c \cdots p_y}$$

and in the model m_2 = ABC:ACD:BCE of Figure 26 they are

$$\rho_{abcde} = p_{abc} \, p_{d|ac} \, p_{e|bc} = \frac{p_{abc} \, p_{acd} \, p_{bce}}{p_{ac} \, p_{bc}}$$

Given that the logarithm of a product equals the sum of the logarithms of each part, the entropies of these probabilities become the sum of the entropies in each component, conditional on the variables shared among them:

$$H(A:B:C:\ldots:Z) = H(A) + H(B) + H(C) + \ldots + H(Z)$$

$$H(AB:BC:\ldots:YZ) = H(AB) + H_B(C) + \ldots + H_Y(Z)$$

$$H(ABC:ACD:BCE) = H(ABC) + H_{AC}(D) + H_{BC}(E)$$

Generalizing from the above, the *maximum entropy* in a model without loops and without structural zeros is

$$H(K_1:K_2:K_3:\ldots) = \sum_e H(K_e) \tag{12.1}$$

$$-\sum_e \sum_{f>e} H(K_e \,\&\, K_f)$$

$$+\sum_e \sum_{f>e} \sum_{g>f} H(K_e \,\&\, K_f \,\&\, K_g)$$

$-$ All entropies in variables shared among four components

$+$ etc.

In words, it is the sum of the entropies in their components minus the sum of the entropies in variables shared by pairs of components, plus the sum of the entropies in variables shared by any three components, minus . . . and so on until no shared variables remain. So for ABC:ACD:BCE,

$$\begin{aligned} H(ABC:ACD:BCE) &= H(ABC) + H(ACD) + H(BCE) \\ &\quad -H(AC) - H(BC) \quad - H(C) \\ &\quad + H(C) \\ &= H(ABC) + H_{BC}(E) + H_{AC}(D) \\ &= H(ACD) + H_{AC}(B) + H_{BC}(E) \\ &= H(BCE) + H_{BC}(A) + H_{AC}(D) \end{aligned}$$

The first of these identities illustrates the entropy computation by 12.1; the last three reflect the orders in which components can be assembled sequentially. For comparing models without loops and without structural zeros, information quantities can also be expressed as mere entropy differences:

$$I(m_i \rightarrow m_j) = H(m_j) - H(m_i) \tag{12.2}$$

Although the transmission measures of information theory were originally developed for models of independent variables and different covers (McGill, 1954; Ashby, 1969), all of which are naturally loopless, 12.1 and 12.2 point to the possibility of finding **T**-measures for the informational differences between descendent models. Consider the models depicted in Figure 24 for examples. The closest common ancestor of m_i and m_j has a loop and cannot be considered here, but the remaining models in this figure are loopless. Illustrating the above, the amount of information $\mathbf{I}(m_j \rightarrow m_i \cap m_j)$ can be simplified using 12.1, 12.2, and 4.4 for the last step:

$$\begin{aligned} \mathbf{H}(A:BD:CD:CE) &= \mathbf{H}(A) + \mathbf{H}(BD) + \mathbf{H}(CD) + \mathbf{H}(CE) \\ &\quad - \mathbf{H}(D) - \mathbf{H}(C) \\ -\mathbf{H}(ABD:CD:CE) &= \quad - \mathbf{H}(ABD) - \mathbf{H}(CD) - \mathbf{H}(CE) \\ &\quad + \mathbf{H}(D) + \mathbf{H}(C) \\ \hline \mathbf{I}(ABD:CD:CE \rightarrow A:BD:CD:CE) &= \mathbf{H}(A) + \mathbf{H}(BD) - \mathbf{H}(ABD) \\ &= \mathbf{I}(ABD \rightarrow A:BD) = \mathbf{T}(A:BD) \end{aligned}$$

The algebraic properties of information in loopless models are further developed in Chapter 13.

Models With Loops or With Structural Zeros

The very nature of loops is that the components involved ultimately affect themselves. Loops have neither beginning nor end. The distribution of probabilities generated by models with loops must reflect this crucial circularity. Entropies cannot be obtained by (closed form) algebraic expressions that imply a linear order of computation. Take the model AB:BC:AC for example. Applying the first component AB to the observed probabilities p_a, we compute probabilities p_b and, applying the second component BC to these, we find p_c. But then, applying the third component AC, which closes the circle, we obtain values for p'_a that may not be the same as those with which we started, requiring revisions, revisions of revisions, and so on. To take appropriate account of this circularity, the computation has to proceed as indicated by such a model and go around and around its loops until the distribution achieves equilibrium (i.e., $\omega_{abc...z} = \omega'_{abc...z}$) and is maximum in entropy. The iterative algorithm described below does just this.

It happens that structural zeros may make similar computational demands. For example, in Figure 29 we find a matrix with structural zeros in the diagonal. Had all cells of this matrix been occupiable, the probabilities expected under the null hypothesis of independence would have been $\pi_{ab} = p_a p_b$. However, this expression assigns non-zero expectations also to the diagonal, yields an entropy that exceeds the maximum obtainable within that matrix, and is thus misleading. Suppose, then, we acknowledge the structural zeros and adjust the expected probabilities in the non-zero cells by $\pi'_{ab} = p_a p_b (1 - p_b)$. Although the columns now add up, $\sum_a \pi'_{ab} = p_b$, the rows do not, $\sum_b \pi'_{ab} \neq p_a$. Attempting to adjust π'_{ab} further so that also the row sums conform to the required marginal values now disturbs the column sums, and so on, again forcing the computation into a seemingly unending cycle of revisions similar to models with loops.

Although there are several cases of matrices with structural zeros that can be evaluated by conventional algebraic methods (see Bishop et al., 1978, and the triangular matrix in Figure 29 for examples), the steps involved are often so cumbersome that we suggest using the iterative algorithm in all of these cases.

We state the *iterative algorithm*, originally proposed by Demming and Stephan and generalized by Darroch and Ratcliff (1972), in these terms:

Given a model $K_1 : K_2 : \ldots : K_r$ with r components K_e.

Let $p_{abc\ldots}$ be the observed probabilities in the space ABC . . . the model covers.

Let p_{k_e} be the probabilities in the eth component K_e, obtained by summing over the values $\bar{k}_e \epsilon \bar{K}_e$ of K_e's complement (variables not in K_e):

$$p_{k_e} = \sum_{\bar{k}_e} p_{abc\ldots}$$

Let N_0 be the number of structural zeros, N_f be the number of fixed probabilities and let v be the sum of the fixed probabilities.

Set the N_0 cells with structural zeros to: $\omega^{(0)}_{abc\ldots} = 0$

Set the N_f cells with fixed probabilities to: $\omega^{(0)}_{abc\ldots} = p_{abc\ldots}$

Set the remaining $N_{ABC\ldots} - N_0 - N_f$ cells to: $\omega^{(0)}_{abc\ldots} = (1 - v)/(N_{ABC} - N_0 - N_f)$

For iterations: $t = 0, 1, 2, \ldots$

For components: K_e, $e = 1, 2, 3, \ldots, r$

For cells whose $N_{ABC\ldots} - N_0 - N_f$ cells are to be computed

$$\omega^{(rt+e)}_{abc\ldots} = p_{k_e} \frac{\omega^{(rt+e-1)}_{abc\ldots}}{\sum_{\bar{k}_e} \omega^{(rt+e-1)}_{abc\ldots}}$$

Stop when a suitable level of approximation is reached.

In words and exemplified by a model AB:BC:AC in, say, a $2 \times 4 \times 3$ space ABC without structural zeros, we start with the parameters of this model, the probabilities p_{ab}, p_{bc}, and p_{ac}, obtained by summing over values in C, in A, and in B, respectively. These marginal probabilities must be satisfied by the distribution we seek to generate. As there are neither structural zeros nor fixed cell entries, we initialize $\omega_{abc} = 1/24$ in each of the $2 \times 4 \times 3$ cells. Then:

We obtain the marginal probabilities in AB by:

$$\omega_{ab}^{(3t)} = \sum_{c} \omega_{abc}^{(3t)}$$

Considering that ω_{ab} should equal p_{ab}, we adjust:

$$\omega_{abc}^{(3t+1)} = p_{ab} \frac{\omega_{abc}^{(3t)}}{\omega_{ab}^{(3t)}}$$

We obtain the marginal probabilities in BC by:

$$\omega_{bc}^{(3t+1)} = \sum_{a} \omega_{abc}^{(3t+1)}$$

Considering that ω_{bc} should equal p_{bc}, we adjust:

$$\omega_{abc}^{(3t+2)} = p_{bc} \frac{\omega_{abc}^{(3t+1)}}{\omega_{bc}^{(3t+1)}}$$

We obtain the marginal probabilities in AC by:

$$\omega_{ac}^{(3t+2)} = \sum_{b} \omega_{abc}^{(3t+2)}$$

Considering that ω_{ac} should equal p_{ac}, we adjust:

$$\omega_{abc}^{(3t+3)} = p_{ac} \frac{\omega_{abc}^{(3t+2)}}{\omega_{ac}^{(3t+2)}}$$

We increment t by 1 and continue until the computed probabilities ω_{k_e} in each component K_e approximates the observed probabilities p_{k_e} within desired limits.

For models with simple loops and only a few structural zeros or fixed probabilities, a reasonable approximation to the maximum entropy distribution is found in five to eight iterations, after which probabilities are generally accurate in the first three digits. When models contain neither loops nor structural zeros, the algorithm achieves a perfect fit after the first iteration. With the availability of computers, the iterative algorithm therefore may be used to compute the maximum entropy probabilities for all models. A test for having reached a reasonably close approximation then obviates the test for the presence of loops presented in Chapter 7. Although algebraic expressions are undoubtedly useful conceptually and advantageous computationally, the iterative algorithm is entirely general and limited only by the computability of the space ABC...Z, specifically by its size $N_{ABC...Z}$.

13. CONFIRMATION

In a confirmatory mode of analysis, we start with a structural model, then test how well that model fits the given data, and, finally, we analyze the details of the model's fit to direct the interpretation of findings. In contrast, in an exploratory mode, we specify at most the properties of the class of models to be considered and leave the search for an optimum model (in a sense to be delineated) to a procedure, usually in the form of a computer algorithm. The confirmatory approach is particularly appropriate when the analysis is guided by theoretical considerations—for example, when the validity of a particular theory is at stake or when some patterns of explanation are preferable to others.

We will elaborate here several analytical devices applicable to structural models generally and leave the search algorithms for Chapter 14.

The Goodness of Fit of a Model

The goodness of fit reduces to testing the significance of the difference between the original data in the saturated model m_o and the distribution generated by a model m_j that conforms to the data only in its parameters and is maximum in entropy otherwise (see Figure 19). According to 8.4, in which m_o is represented by the observed probabilities $p_{abc...z}$ and m_j by the generated probabilities $\rho_{abc...z}$, the amount of information by which the model is in error is

$$I(m_o \rightarrow m_j) = \sum p_{abc..} \log_2 \frac{p_{abc..}}{\rho_{abc..}}$$

A zero value of this quantity indicates a perfect fit. Non-zero values are tested for their significance, using 11.1:

$$\mathbf{L}^2_{m_o \to m_j} = 1.3863\ n\ \mathbf{I}(m_o \to m_j)$$

in which n is the sample size. Together with the appropriate degrees of freedom $\mathbf{df}_{m_o \to m_j}$, as discussed in Chapter 10, and an ordinary χ^2 table, the significance level is determined as in Chapter 11. In this test the whole model acts as a structural null hypothesis. If the quantity by which the model is in error is significant, then the model must be rejected as inadequate. If this quantity is insignificant, the model may be accepted as an explanation of the data, its significance level indicating the probability of being wrong in this decision.

The Amount of Information Modeled

This assesses the difference between the distribution generated by the model in hand and the distribution that would be expected if all of the model's variables were unrelated or independent. With the observed probabilities $p_{abc...z}$ in m_o, the probabilities $\rho_{abc...z}$ generated by m_j as in the above, but with the probability $\pi_{abc...z}$ associated with the model m_{ind}, the amount of information modeled is

$$\mathbf{I}(m_j \to m_{ind}) = \sum p_{abc..} \log_2 \frac{\rho_{abc..}}{\pi_{abc..}}$$

For a model to be a reasonably good one we expect this quantity to be large. If it is not, a significance test in which m_{ind} serves as the structural null hypothesis will reveal whether the modeling effort has merit at all.

The two information quantities are related by 8.5:

$$\mathbf{I}(m_o \to m_{ind}) = \mathbf{I}(m_o \to m_j) + \mathbf{I}(m_j \to m_{ind})$$

which suggests two instructive expressions, indicating the proportion of information a model explains or fails to account for, respectively:

Proportion of unexplained information	$\mathbf{I}(m_o \to m_j)/\mathbf{I}(m_o \to m_{ind})$
Proportion of explained information	$\mathbf{I}(m_j \to m_{ind})/\mathbf{I}(m_o \to m_{ind})$

For example, the model m_j = EAE′:EAA′ for the television and aggression data in Figure 5, also depicted in Figure 35, is evaluated as follows:

Information Ignored	*Information Modeled*
$\mathbf{I}(m_o \rightarrow m_j) = .0080$ bits	$\mathbf{I}(m_j \rightarrow m_{ind}) = .6229$ bits
$\mathbf{L}^2 = 3.35$	$\mathbf{L}^2 = 262.53$
df = 4	**df** = 7
significance = no	significance = .0001 level
unexplained = 1.27%	explained = 98.73%

These rather unambiguous findings suggest that it would be a mistake to dismiss the model relating prior TV violence exposure, E, and prior aggressive behavior, A, to subsequent TV violence exposure, E′, on the one hand and to subsequent aggressive behavior, A′, on the other. However, the confidence this test establishes refers only to the absence of modeling errors. Neither the test nor any of the measures employed will indicate whether the model is structurally the most economical one, an issue discussed in Chapter 14. Moreover, these measures apply only to a *model as a whole* and are not indicative of its individual parts, to which we will now turn.

The Complexity of a Model's Components

This should indicate how much is involved in describing or in building a model's components. Whether a component operationalizes a verbal hypothesis or embodies a complex function, in order to contribute to the modeling effort that component must recognize or draw a finite number of distinctions. The larger this number is, the more variety it can store, transmit, or share and the more difficult it will therefore be to describe or materially represent that component. The *required number of cells* or states ranges between the following extremes:

$$] \, 2^{\mathbf{H}(K)} \, [\leqslant \begin{matrix}\text{required number}\\ \text{of states or cells}\end{matrix} \leqslant N_K \qquad [13.1]$$

where N_K is the number of occupiable cells in K, excluding structural zeros, **H**(K) is the entropy in K, and the inverted brackets denote that the enclosed expression is to be rounded to the nearest larger integer. $\log_2$ of the three expressions would give the complexity of a component in bits.

The Contributions a Component Makes

A model's contributions to the amount of information modeled are of two kinds, *unique* to a component and *shared* with other components of that model. Both quantities add up to the *total* amount of information processed by the component in question. All of these contributions are obtained by removing certain interactions from a component and measuring the informational difference this makes.

The interactions that need to be removed from a component K are absent in the partition K_{part} of this component's variables into sets of *variables that always cooccur* in the model. For example, in Figure 33, AB and CD always occur together in $K_1:K_2:K_3$ = ABCDE:CDEF:EFG. Partitioning K_1 by this rule yields K_{1part} = AB:CD:E in which AB are variables unique to K_1 and partitioning K_3 yields K_{3part} = E:F:G in which G is unique to K_3. The latter omits the interactions <EF>, <EFG>, <EG>, <FG>, of which <EF> is shared by K_2 and K_3, the other three being unique to K_3.

The *total amount of information processed* by a component is the informational difference between the whole and the partitioned component and makes no reference to the context of that component. Given that the partitioned component consists of independent variables, we can express this quantity in two ways:

$$\mathbf{I}(K \rightarrow K_{part}) = \mathbf{T}(K_{part}) \tag{13.2}$$

In the preceding example, K_1 processes **I**(ABCDE→AB:CD:E) = **T**(AB:CD:E) bits.

The *unique contribution* by a component is the informational difference between the model m that contains the component K whole and the model m,K_{part} that contains K_{part} in K's place:

$$\mathbf{I}(m \rightarrow m, K_{part}) \tag{13.3}$$

In practice, because all but K's unique variables are shared with other components in the model m and are hence redundant in m,K_{part}, the model m,K_{part} represents K by its unique variables only and is simply omitted if no such variables exist. The component K_1 of the model in Figure 33 contains the unique variable AB, whereas K_2 contains none. Their unique contributions are, respectively,

$$\mathbf{I}(m \rightarrow m, K_{1part}) = \mathbf{I}(ABCDE : CDEF : EFG \rightarrow AB : CDEF : EFG)$$

$$\mathbf{I}(m \rightarrow m, K_{2part}) = \mathbf{I}(ABCDE : CDEF : EFG \rightarrow ABCDE : EFG)$$

In a component's unique contribution, the variables shared with the other components of that model are *controlled*, averaged over all of their values and thereby prevented from entering that measure, whereas in the total amount of information processed by a component, variables are

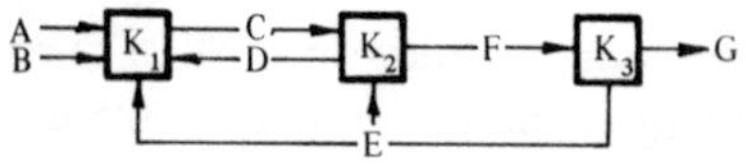

ABCDE : CDEF : EFG

Figure 33

not controlled and may hence contain shared, or what is sometimes called spurious, quantities.

The amount of *information shared* between one component K and all other components of the model m is the difference between K's total quantity and its unique contribution:

$$\mathbf{I}(K \rightarrow K_{part}) - \mathbf{I}(m \rightarrow m, K_{part}) \qquad [13.4]$$

In models without loops, these contributions can be expressed by **T**-measures. Figure 34 differentiates the contributions for the model in Figure 33. For example, the amount of information **T**(E:F) that responds to the interaction <EF> contained in both K_2 and K_3 is a shared quantity, could be processed in either of the two components, and contributes to the totals of both. The shared quantity **T**(CD:E) could be similarly handled, either in K_1 or in K_2. Naturally, the unique quantities respond only to interactions unique to a component. An example of a model without shared contributions is the chain AB:BC:CD:...:YZ. Only when shared contributions are absent do the contributions made by individual components add to the total amount a model processes. This sum is uninterpretable otherwise.

The Strength of Relations (Association)

The strength of relations within a model's components follows from the above. Association is strongest when (a) all variables attached to a component are perfectly predictable (determined) from each other and

Model:	K_1 ABCDE	:	K_2 CDEF	:	K_3 EFG
Unique Contributions					
$\mathbf{I}(m \rightarrow m, K_{part})$	**T**(AB : CDE)		**T**(CDE : EF)		**T**(EF : G)
Shared Contributions					
$\mathbf{I}(K \rightarrow K_{part}) - \mathbf{I}(m \rightarrow m, K_{part})$	**T**(CD : E)		**T**(CD : E) + **T**(E : F)		**T**(E : F)
Totals $\mathbf{I}(K \rightarrow K_{part})$	**T**(AB : CD : E)		**T**(CD : E : F)		**T**(E : F : G)

Figure 34

(b) the component realizing this relation is essential in the context of all other components of that model. The bivariate index of predictability introduced in the form of 4.9 responds to condition a and is a qualitative analogue of the path coefficient or the squared correlation coefficient. We need to generalize this index to any structure and hence to numbers of variables larger than two, thus making it responsive to condition b.

The measure of a component's unique contribution is sensitive to the network of connections in which that component participates and serves as an *absolute* measure of association among its variables. The upper limit of this quantity is found with 8.9, and the proportion of the two quantities indicates the extent to which a component's behavior is predictable or determinate (as opposed to governed by random processes). We propose the following *relative measure of association* as a generalization of 4.9:

$$0 \leqslant t_{K,m} = \frac{\mathbf{I}(m \to m, K_{part})}{\mathbf{I}(m \to m, K_{part})_{max}} \leqslant 1 \qquad [13.5]$$

$\mathbf{t}_{K,m}$ (read the subscript as "component K in the context of model m") indicates the strength of the associations within K. These associations are unique to K, not shared with other components of the model m. The index is zero when the variables separated in $\mathbf{K}_{part}$ are all independent in K, in which case K is a totally fictitious component of m and may be omitted without loss. The index is unity when the variables in $\mathbf{K}_{part}$ are within the confines of the model's parameters maximally constrained, in which case K embodies a many-to-one if not a one-to-one-to-one . . . relation (the qualitative analogue of perfect "multicollinearity" and the multivariate version of perfect correlation).

Applied to the television and aggression data in Figure 5, the unique contribution of the component EAE′ of the model EAE′:EAA′ in Figure 35 that attempts to explain TV exposure to violence is

$$\mathbf{I}(m \to m, K_{part}) = \mathbf{I}(EAE' : EAA' \to E' : EAA') = .2032$$

With $\mathbf{L}^2 = 85.6$ and $\mathbf{df} = 3$ this contribution is significant at the .0001 level. Its maximum is obtained by 8.9:

$$\begin{aligned} \mathbf{I}(m \to m, K_{part})_{max} &= \mathbf{I}(m \to m, K_{part}) + \mathbf{H}(EAE') - \max[\mathbf{H}(E'), \mathbf{H}(EA)] \\ &= \quad .2032 \quad + 2.7922 \quad - \max[.9992, 1.9962] \\ &= .9992 \end{aligned}$$

Thus the association coefficient becomes $\mathbf{t}_{EAE', EAE':EAA'} = .2032/.9992 = .2034$. It suggests that the association in EAE′, though statistically significant, has only 20% of the strength it could have within the context of this model. This value is found in the appropriate box in Figure 35, which also depicts the model EE′:EA′:AA′ for comparison.

With reference to the latter model in this figure, exposure to violent TV programming and aggressive behavior turns out to be remarkably stable over time, with television exerting only a small influence on aggressive behavior. In assessing such associations it is important to note that the choice of a model is crucial because it specifies the controls to which measures of a component's strength respond. Associations like those discussed could be spurious, an issue we will now address.

The Amount of Interaction

This is the informational difference between two models that differ only by the interaction to be assessed, one being the immediate descendent of the other. For example, the model ABC:ABD:CD includes the interaction <CD>, whereas the model ABC:ABD does not, the latter being an immediate descendent of the former. The model ABC:ABD includes the interaction <ABC>, whereas AC:BC:ABD does not, both being exactly one generation apart. With this understanding the amount of interaction is merely notational. Let $m\overline{<K>}$ be a model that excludes the interaction <K> and let m <K> be the *immediate ancestor* of $m\overline{<K>}$, now including <K>. The amount of information associated with the interaction <K> then becomes

$$\mathbf{I}(m<K> \rightarrow m\overline{<K>}) \qquad [13.6]$$

With reference to the model m_o, this quantity is called the *genuine* (as opposed to the spurious) *amount of interaction* for it expresses the amount of information in interaction <K> with *all* variables *not in* K *controlled* for, averaged, or prevented from contributing to this measure. References to models other than m_o omit some of these

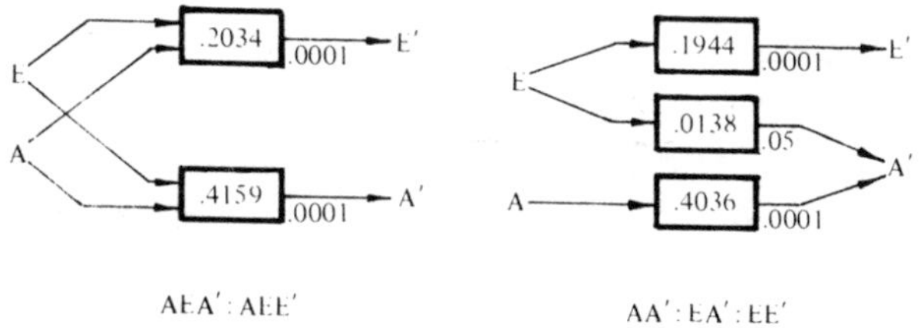

Figure 35

controls. Figure 36 shows genuine interactions of different ordinality and controls within five variables.

Continuing the example of the television and aggression data, the extent of the multiple causal relations among television exposure, aggression, and subsequent aggression—that is, the amount of genuine interaction in <EAA′>—is

$$\mathbf{I}(EAE' : EAA' : EE'A' : AE'A' \rightarrow EAE' : EE'A' : AE'A') = .0008$$

and is not significant. The extent to which exposure to television violence causes aggression—that is, the amount of genuine interaction in <EA′>—is

$$\mathbf{I}(EAE' : EA' : AE'A' \rightarrow EAE' : AE'A') = .0058$$

It is larger than the triple interaction but still not significant. However, the stability of aggressive behavior—that is, the amount of genuine interaction in <AA′>:

$$\mathbf{I}(EAE' : AA' : EE'A' \rightarrow EAE' : EE'A') = .3869$$

yields $\mathbf{L}^2$ = 163.1, **df** = 1, and is significant at the .0001 level. This interaction cannot be dismissed. Thus interaction effects can be isolated and measured with the strongest controls to which given data lend themselves. As we said, weaker controls are possible in the context of models other than m_o.

Strata Within Models

Structural models may be examined from yet another perspective. One always can ignore some of the variables of a multivariate distribution by summing and then test models with smaller covers on the *whole sample*. But one can also leave the dimensionality of the data intact and examine how well a model fits within a particular *subsample*

Ordinality	<K>	m_o <K>	$m_o\overline{\langle K\rangle}$	<K> Controlled By
5	<ABCDE>	ABCDE = m_o	ABCD : ABCE : ABDE : ACDE : BCDE	none
4	<ABCD>	ABCD : ABCE : ABDE : ACDE : BCDE	ABCE : ABDE : ACDE : BCDE	E
3	<ABC>	ABC : ABDE : ACDE : BCDE	ABDE : ACDE : BCDE	DE
2	<AB>	AB : ACDE : BCDE	ACDE : BCDE	CDE

Figure 36

of these data. When such subsamples are defined in a model's own terms, one evaluates strata within a space.

For example, in a model that suggests a certain variable to be the input or the controlling variable of the modeled process, one may want to test the extent to which the behavior of the model associated with each input value conforms to or deviates from the structure summarily represented by the model of all data. If the input to such a model is an on-off switch, causing a structure in the on position and independence in the alternative, the model would presumably be confirmed in the on position only, data on the off position then merely add noise. Or consider a complex model of social mobility, including categories of religious affiliations. It is quite possible that each religious group conforms to a variation of the general model and that a separate assessment of their conformity to the descendents of this general model might provide additional insights about the differences among these groups.

Information measures aiding the examination of strata take advantage of the fact that information quantities are averages of log-likelihood ratios as in 4.7 and that such averages may also be obtained for any subspace of a multivariate space characterized by particular values in its variables or in the parameters of a model. We generalize the informational bias 5.2 to complex models:

$$\mathbf{I}(m_i \rightarrow m_j) = \sum_s p_s \, \mathbf{I}_s(m_i \rightarrow m_j) \qquad [13.7]$$

and

$$\mathbf{I}_s(m_i \rightarrow m_j) = \frac{1}{p_s} \sum_{\bar{s}} p_{s\bar{s}} \log_2 \frac{\omega_{s\bar{s}}}{\rho_{s\bar{s}}} \qquad [13.8]$$

where s denotes one category or value of a subspace S of ABC...Z covered by the two models m_i and m_j, $\bar{s}$ is a category or values of S's complement $\bar{S}$ in ABC...Z, probabilities $p_{s\bar{s}} = p_{abc...z}$ are observed, probabilities $\omega_{s\bar{s}} = \omega_{abc...z}$ are generated by m_i, and probabilities $\rho_{s\bar{s}} = \rho_{abc...z}$ are generated by m_j. Equation 13.7 partitions an information quantity into the weighted sum of the information quantities associated with each stratum s, and 13.8 shows the latter as the average log-likelihood ratio within that stratum.

We follow the notational conventions of 5.2 according to which the stratum s, which is indicated by subscript in the above, replaces references to those variables in the model designations, now held constant:

$$\mathbf{I}_a(\mathrm{AB} \to \mathrm{A:B}) = \mathbf{I}(\mathrm{aB} \to \mathrm{a:B}) = \mathbf{T}(\mathrm{a:B})$$

$$= \frac{1}{p_a} \sum_b p_{ab} \log_2 \frac{p_{ab}}{\pi_{ab}}$$

in which case the degrees of freedom is not $\mathbf{df}_{AB \to A:B}$ but $\mathbf{df}_B$. Using ABC:BD:CD and AB:C:D as examples, we can examine *any slice* (hyperplane) in the multivariate space by holding one value constant—for example, in the unique variable A:

$$\mathbf{I}_a(\mathrm{ABC:BD:CD} \to \mathrm{AB:C:D}) = \mathbf{I}(\mathrm{aBC:BD:CD} \to \mathrm{aB:C:D})$$

$$= \frac{1}{p_a} \sum_{bcd} p_{abcd} \log_2 \frac{\omega_{abcd}}{\rho_{abcd}}$$

for which the degree of freedom becomes $\mathbf{df}_{BC:BD:CD \to B:C:D}$. We can examine *any parameter* of a model (subspace or cylinder of the multivariate space) by holding one of its values constant—for example, in the second component:

$$\mathbf{I}_{bd}(\mathrm{ABC:BD:CD} \to \mathrm{AB:C:D}) = \mathbf{I}(\mathrm{AbC:bd:Cd} \to \mathrm{Ab:C:d})$$

$$= \frac{1}{p_{bd}} \sum_{ac} p_{abcd} \log_2 \frac{\omega_{abcd}}{\rho_{abcd}}$$

whereby the degree of freedom reduces to $\mathbf{df}_{AC \to A:C}$. And in the extreme case, we can examine *any state* of the model (a cell in the multivariate space):

$$\mathbf{I}_{abcd}(\mathrm{ABC:BD:CD} \to \mathrm{AB:C:D}) = \mathbf{I}(\mathrm{abc:bd:cd} \to \mathrm{ab:c:d})$$

$$= \log_2 \frac{\omega_{abcd}}{\rho_{abcd}}$$

losing all degrees of freedom, however. The latter is no longer an information measure proper but will identify deviant cells. We exemplified its use in Figure 15.

The reduction in the number of degrees of freedom points to the fact that strata are not capable of recognizing the highest-order interaction in the original data. Tests on strata of models are particularly useful in conjunction with forms like 8.5, which partitions the total amount of information into the amount omitted and represented by that model. Equation 13.7 points to the possibility of aggregating the individual strata similar to the informational bias in Figure 17.

14. EXPLORATION

In an exploratory mode of analysis we search among models that possess certain specified structural properties to find those with an optimal balance between the two conflicting criteria of simplicity and goodness of fit. Inasmuch as the search presupposes little about the data under consideration, exploration may lead to unanticipated results. We will illustrate the process by means of several algorithms.

Searching for the Ordinalities of Appropriate Models

Data may vary greatly in complexity. Appropriate techniques for analysis must have the capacity to respond to their complexity or potentially important patterns may never be discovered. Here we search for the ordinality of the interactions manifest in multivariate data.

As a digression, we note that most of the familiar statistical techniques in the social sciences respond to binary relations only and are then of ordinality two: correlations between pairs of variables, similarities and distances between observations, networks of communication links between senders and receivers, comparisons between two systems, and so on. Such techniques are computationally convenient, but if there are reasons to suspect that higher-order interactions are present in the data, one should at least ascertain the significance of omitting these. The appropriate measure of this omission is the informational difference between the original data m_o and a model consisting of all possible binary components AB:AC:AD:...:YZ. It assesses the interaction of ordinality larger than two.

Using the superscript w to denote the common ordinality of the components of a model, starting with $m^W = m_o$, where W is the number of variables covered by m_o and also the largest ordinality these data may contain, and ending with the model consisting of W independent variables, $m^1 = m_{ind}$, we partition the total amount of information in the data $\mathbf{I}(m^W \rightarrow m^1) = \mathbf{I}(m_o \rightarrow m_{ind})$ by

$$I(m^{W} \to m^{W-1}) = \text{amount of W-th order interaction} \qquad [14.1]$$

$$I(m^{W-1} \to m^{W-2}) = \text{amount of W}-1\text{-th order interaction}$$

$$\vdots$$

$$I(m^{w} \to m^{w-1}) = \text{amount of w-th order interaction}$$

$$\vdots$$

$$I(m^{3} \to m^{2}) = \text{amount of third-order interaction}$$

$$I(m^{2} \to m^{1}) = \text{amount of second-order interaction}$$

For example, for the five variables A, B, C, E, and F (omitting D) of data in Figure 28, we obtain the following account:

$$\begin{aligned} I(m^5 \to m^4) &= .0000 \\ I(m^4 \to m^3) &= .9780 \\ I(m^3 \to m^2) &= .0000 \\ I(m^2 \to m^1) &= .0743 \\ \hline I(m^5 \to m^1) &= 1.0523 \text{ bits} \end{aligned}$$

where:

m^5 = ABCEF

m^4 = ABCE : ABCF : ABEF : ACEF : BCEF

m^3 = ABC : ABE : ABF : ACE : ACF : AEF : BCE : BCF : BEF : CEF

m^2 = AB : AC : AE : AF : BC : BE : BF : CE : CF : EF

m^1 = A : B : C : E : F

Here interactions of ordinality two amount to only .0743 bits, or 7% of the total amount of information in the data. Interactions of ordinality four measure .9780 bits and account for the remaining 93%. All tertiary and quintenary interactions are absent. The account suggests that an analysis of the data in terms of pairs of variables would miss the most important pattern and that an appropriate analytical technique should respond to pattern of an ordinality of at least four. Thus the researcher locates the ordinality of the interactional content in given data and is able to determine the requirements of appropriate analytical techniques.

Note that all models with components of uniform ordinality larger than unity possess loops and require iterative procedures and hence electronic computers for their evaluation. Note further that the number of components of an ordinality of w is $W!/w!(W-w)!$, increases with the number W of variables covered by the model, and is additionally largest when w = W/2. These numbers can easily exceed computational limits and must be kept small in practical applications. Because analytical techniques of lower ordinality are more readily available and easier to apply, we suggest evaluating such models in the order of their increasing ordinality—that is, first m^1, then m^2, then ^{3}, and so on—until either practical analytical procedures of that ordinality are no longer available or satisfactory amounts of information are accounted for. Exceeding the former criterion suggests that the data are too complex to be analyzed; reaching the latter conditions indicates the ordinality an appropriate technique would require. For other heuristics see Conant (1981).

Searching for Optimum Models

Here we describe a general search algorithm for data explorations and in turn develop three variations of this procedure. The steps in this general algorithm are

(1) Start with some model m_i (this model could be the saturated model m_o containing all complexities in the data, the model m^W as obtained from the previous procedure, or any model suggested in theoretical writings, for example).

(2) Compute the next generation of descendents m_j of the model m_i that conforms to the desired characteristics of the models to be explored. (The implementation of the algorithm varies with these characteristics.)

(3) For each descendent model m_j compute $\mathbf{I}(m_i \rightarrow m_j)$, $\mathbf{I}(m_o \rightarrow m_j)$, their statistical significance, or whatever may serve as a termination criterion for the search process.

(4) Unless a termination criterion is reached, enter the (set of) model(s) m_j for which $\mathbf{I}(m_i \rightarrow m_j)$ is smallest as the next ancestor(s) of m_i into step 2 above. The most obvious termination criterion is that the quantity $\mathbf{I}(m_o \rightarrow m_j)$ of information omitted is statistically significant. Another criterion is that the quantity $\mathbf{I}(m_o \rightarrow m_j)$ exceeds a certain proportion of the total $\mathbf{I}(m_o \rightarrow m_{ind})$, and so on.

Essentially the algorithm calls for computing the next generation of descendents of a given model, selecting the model(s) with the smallest error (best fit) from these and reapplying the algorithm on the model(s) selected until structural simplifications are no longer justifiable. Now consider three implementations of this search.

General models with same covers. In this approach variables are neither differentiated by kind nor assumed to have an a priori ordering.

All structural models are considered possible except that each model accounts for the same variables selected for analysis; no variable is discarded. The following algorithm in place of step 2 generates all immediate descendents:

Given a model $m_i = \mathbf{K}_1:\mathbf{K}_2:\ldots:\mathbf{K}_r$ or r components $\mathbf{K}_f$.

Let the component K_f have w variables $V', V'', \ldots, V^w$

For each K_f, $f = 1, 2, \ldots, r$, for which $w > 1$, generate an immediate descendent as follows:

(a) Replace K_f by the string $K_f - V':K_f - V'':\ldots:K_f - V^w$ in which each $K - V$ omits a different variable, thus eliminating the interaction $\langle K_f \rangle$ from K_f.

(b) Remove any $K - V$ that is now redundant relative to the remainder of m_i and enter the result as an immediate descendent m_j.

The resulting set of models m_j is the set of immediate descendents of the model m_i.

For example, m_i = ABC:CD. Decomposing the first component yields AB:AC:BC:CD without redundancies. Decomposing the second component yields ABC:C:D in which C is redundant. Hence ABC:CD's two immediate descendents are AB:AC:BC:CD and ABC:D. The former omits the interaction <ABC>, the latter omits the interaction <CD>.

When this algorithm for generating immediate descendents of a model is entered in step 2 of the general search algorithm and applied to the election data in Figure 3, the search proceeds as shown in Figure 37.

Here A and A′ are party affiliations (R = Republican, D = Democrat) obtained during the first and second interview, respectively, and P and P′ are preferences (+, –) for Willkie expressed at the same two times. The models with the smallest error in any one generation are starred (asterisk) in the righthand column of Figure 37 and taken to be the ancestor(s) of the models generated at the subsequent step. Tracing the sequence(s) of models with the smallest errors, we can see that the fourth-order interaction <APA′P′> is removed in step 1, all four third-order interactions are then removed in steps 2 through 5, and three second-order interactions, <AP′>, <PA′>, and <AP> are removed in steps 6 through 8, yielding the model AA′:PP′:A′P′ as the simplest model with still insignificant errors. In all further simplifications errors would become incrementally significant, hence the search may have to stop there. The remaining components generate an artificial distribution that closely approximates the original data. Figure 38 depicts the observed and

Step	Model m_j	$\mathbf{I}(m_o \rightarrow m_j)$	Sig.	$\mathbf{I}(m_{j-1} \rightarrow m_j)$	Sig.	Next Ancestor
0	APA′P′	.0000				
1	APA′ : APP′ : AA′P′ : PA′P′ = m^3	.0001	ns	.0001	ns	*
2	APA′ : APP′ : AA′P′	.0002	ns	.0001	ns	
	APA′ : APP′ : PA′P′	.0001	ns	.0000	ns	*
	APA′ : AA′P′ : PA′P′	.0001	ns	.0000	ns	*
	APP′ : AA′P′ : PA′P′	.0001	ns	.0000	ns	*
3	AA′ : APP′ : PA′P′	.0001	ns	.0000	ns	*
	APA′ : AP′ : PA′P′	.0001	ns	.0000	ns	*
	APA′ : APP′ : A′P′	.0007	ns	.0006	ns	
	AP : AA′P′ : PA′P′	.0001	ns	.0000	ns	*
	APA′ : AA′P′ : PP′	.0019	ns	.0018	ns	
	APP′ : AA′P′ : PA	.0007	ns	.0006	ns	
4	APP′ : PA′P′	.4669	.0001	.4668	.0001	
	AA′ : AP : AP′ : PA′P′	.0001	ns	.0000	ns	*
	AA′ : APP′ : PA′ : A′P′	.0008	ns	.0007	ns	
	APA′ : PA′P′	.0020	ns	.0019	ns	
	APA′ : AP′ : PP′ : A′P′	.0019	ns	.0018	ns	
	AA′P′ : PA′P′	.0192	ns	.0191	.0100	
	AP : AA′P′ : PA′ : PP′	.0019	ns	.0018	ns	

5	AA′ : AP′ : PA′P′	.0193	ns	.0192	.0100	
	AP : AP′ : PA′P′	.4685	.0001	.4684	.0001	
	AP : AA′ : PA′P′	.0020	ns	.0019	ns	
	AP : AA′ : AP′ : PA′ : PP′ : A′P′ = m^2	.0019	ns	.0018	ns	*
6	AP : AA′ : AP′ : PA′ : PP·	.0460	.0100	.0441	.0001	
	AP : AA′ : AP′ : PA′ : A′P′	.2799	.0001	.2780	.0001	
	AP : AA′ : AP′ : PP′ : A′P′	.0178	ns	.0159	ns	
	AP : AA′ : PA′ : PP′ : A′P′	.0040	ns	.0021	ns	*
	AP : AP′ : PA′ : PP′ : A′P′	.4705	.0001	.4686	.0001	
	AA′ : AP′ : PA′ : PP′ : A′P′	.0212	ns	.0193	.0100	
7	AP : AA′ : PA′ : PP′	.1595	.0001	.1555	.0001	
	AP : AA′ : PA′ : A′P′	.2820	ns	.2780	.0001	
	AP : AA′ : PP′ : A′P′	.0183	ns	.0143	ns	*
	AP : PA′ : PP′ : A′P′	.5839	.0001	.5799	.0001	
	AA′ : PA′ : PP′ : A′P′	.0233	ns	.0193	.0100	
8	AP : AA′ : PP′	.1599	.0001	.1416	.0001	
	AP : AA′ : A′P′	.2824	.0001	.2641	.0001	
	AP : PP′ : A′P′	.5840	.0001	.5657	.0001	
	AA′ : PP′ : A′P′	**.0234**	**ns**	**.0051**	**ns**	*****
9	A : PP′ : A′P′	.7947	.0001	.7713	.0001	
	AA′ : P : A′P′	.4931	.0001	.4697	.0001	
	AA′ : PP′	.3705	.0001	.3471	.0001	*
10	A : A′ : PP′	1.1418	.0001	.7713	.0001	
	AA′ : P : P′	.8402	.0001	.4697	.0001	*
11	A : P : A′ : P′ = m^1	1.6115	.0001	.7713	.0001	

Figure 37

Components K_i:

AA′

A \ A′	R	D
R	166	4
D	3	93

A′P′

A′ \ P′	+	−
R	142	27
D	15	82

PP′

P \ P′	+	−
+	143	16
−	14	93

Data m_o:
Model m_j:

APA′P′
(AA′ : A′P′ : PP′)

AP \ A′P′	R+	R−	D+	D−
R+	129 (127.0)	3 (3.9)	1 (0.6)	2 (0.5)
R−	11 (12.5)	23 (22.6)	0 (0.0)	1 (2.9)
D+	1 (2.3)	0 (0.1)	12 (13.1)	11 (11.5)
D−	1 (0.2)	1 (0.4)	2 (1.3)	68 (67.1)

Figure 38

model-generated frequency distributions and above it the three parameters of that model.

The substantive conclusion that could be drawn from this result is that voting is marked first by (the stability of) party affiliations, AA′, second and independent of this by (the stability of) individual preferences for a candidate, PP′, and third and also independent of the two by the resulting relation, A′P′ (which shows a tendency for voters to change toward consistency between party affiliation and preferences for that party's candidate). Although AP resembles A′P′, the tendency toward consistency has the effect of polarizing the population; hence A′P′ represents more information than AP and therefore turns up in the model, whereas AP does not. Higher-order explanations are unwarranted here.

Note that the above search for an optimum model started with m_o = APA′P′ and made no assumptions about the data. By taking advantage of the lattice organization of structural models, it evaluated *all* models of the lattice of possible models implicitly. Figure 25 depicted the types of structures involved; the search could proceed from any model, however. For example, had one first determined where significant ordinalities are located, one would have found that interactions of ordinality three and four are insignificant in this case (see m^3 at step 1 and m^2 at step 5 in Figure 37) and starting with m^2 would have yielded the same result with half the computational effort. Or, starting with a model that represents certain theoretical propositions, one could have ascertained whether simplifications of this model are empirically justifiable. In this example the models produced in steps beyond 8 are no longer justifiable in any case.

The algorithm for generating models covering all variables is one of four including algorithms for generating models that are selective about variables and models without loops (Krippendorff, 1982a).

Regression models distinguish between two kinds of variables: criteria or dependent variables and predictor or independent variables. Predictor variables are intended to explain the criterion variables, and structures within the latter are explored only in reference to this aim. Here we consider one criterion variable only. The algorithm for generating such models, now taking the place of step 2 in the general search procedure, is as follows:

Given any regression model $m_i = ZL_1{:}ZL_2{:}\ldots{:}ZL_r{:}L_o$,
where Z is the criterion variable, L_o is the product of all predictor variables, and L_1, L_2, ... are contained in L_o.
The two extreme cases of such models are the saturated model $m_o = ZL_o$, which includes all relations in the data, and $Z{:}L_o$, which excludes all relations between the two kinds of variables.

Let L_f have w variables V', V'',..., V^W.

For each ZL_f of m_i, f = 1, 2,..., r, taking one at a time

(a) Replace ZL_f by the string $L_f - V'{:}L_f - V''{:}\ldots{:}L_f - V^w$ in which each $L - V$ omits a different variable, thus removing the interaction $\langle L_f \rangle$ from ZL_f. If w = 1, $L_f - V$ omits that one variable.

(b) With each $L_f - V$ resulting from (a) associate the criterion variable Z.

(c) Remove any $Z(L_f - V)$ that is now redundant relative to the remainder of m_i and enter the result as a next-generation regression model m_j.

The resulting set of regression models m_j is the set of next-generation descendents of m_i.

We exemplify the steps involved with the television and aggression data used previously. Aggressive behavior A′ is taken as the criterion variable Z, and the three variables E, A, and E′ are taken as the predictor variables for A′. The steps are shown in Figure 39. Here $L_o = EAE'$ is seen

Step	Model m_j	$\mathbf{I}(m_o \rightarrow m_j)$	Sig.	$\mathbf{I}(m_{j-1} \rightarrow m_j)$	Sig.	Next Ancestor
0	A′ EAE′	.0000				
1	A′ EA : A′ EE′ : A′ AE′ : EAE′	.0017	ns	.0017	ns	*
2	A′ EA : A′ EE′ : EAE′	.0017	ns	.0000	ns	*
	A′ EA : A′ AE′ : EAE′	.0069	ns	.0052	ns	
	A′ EE′ : A′ AE′ : EAE′	.0025	ns	.0008	ns	
3	A′ EA : A′ E′ : EAE′	.0071	ns	.0054	ns	
	A′ EE′ : A′ A : EAE′	.0028	ns	.0011	ns	*
4	A′ EE′ : EAE′	.3985	.0001	.3957	.0001	
	A′ E : A′ A : A′ E′ : EAE′	.0083	ns	.0055	ns	*
5	**A′ E : A′ A : EAE′**	**.0092**	**ns**	**.0009**	**ns**	*
	A′ E : A′ E′ : EAE′	.4025	.0001	.3942	.0001	
	A′ A : A′ E′ : EAE′	.0141	ns	.0058	ns	
6	A′ E : EAE′	.4101	.0001	.4009	.0001	
	A′ A : EAE′	.0203	ns	.0111	.0500	*
7	A′ : EAE′	.4239	.0001	.4036	.0001	

Figure 39

to occur as a separate component in each of these models. It accounts for the interactions among the predictor variables unrelated to A′. The remaining components contain interactions involving A′ and subsets of the variables E, A, and E′. The simplest model with the least amount of error turns out to be A′E:A′A:EAE′ and is found in step 5. It relates television violence and aggressive behavior both separately to subsequent aggressive behavior. Step 6 shows that the A′E component, relating television violence to subsequent aggression, is the weakest and its omission would lead to a barely significant error (.05 level), a finding already depicted in Figure 35.

The above algorithm is the simplest one of several other forms for regression analyses (Krippendorff, 1982b) that could focus on different kinds of contributions (cumulative, ordinal, unique, the above contributions being additive), on multiple criterion variables, or on situations in which two or more classes of variables are considered predictors of each other.

Partition models. Partitioning aims at grouping variables into mutually exclusive subsets of minimal statistical dependence. By identifying subsets that are nearly independent, partitioning may point to variables that can be described separately, without loss or with minimal losses and at a substantial reduction in analytical efforts. Partitioning also yields results consistent with the notion of a hierarchy of part-whole distinctions or of subsystem-system relations and serves the common problem of understanding a whole by its "natural" parts. We describe the algorithm as follows:

> Given any model m_i whose components K partition an initial set of variables into mutually exclusive parts. Initially m_i may be the saturated model m_o and ultimately it becomes m_{ind}.
>
> On each component K of m_i that contains more than one variable, apply the general search algorithm with the algorithm for generating all "models" on the path toward an additional bipartition in place of step 2 and replace K by L:M resulting from K's partition.
>
> The algorithm for generating all "models" on the path toward *one* bipartition initially accepts the component K = L:M, proceeds through "models" LS:SM, where S denotes variables shared by the two components and L and M are unique, and terminates with L:M whose parts are mutually exclusive and jointly cover K's original variables.
>
> Let V′ and V″ denote two variables in S and let S – V say that variable V is removed from S.

Initially: for each pair of variables V′ and V″ in K replace K by (K – V′):(K – V″).
All resulting forms LS:SM are initial descendents of K on the path toward its eventual bipartition.

Otherwise: for each variable V of S
replace LS:SM by LS:(S – V)M and by L(S – V):SM
The resulting forms are subsequent descendents of K on the path toward its eventual bipartition.

The lattice in Figure 40 contains all possible structures of models on the path toward one bipartition of seven variables. The number of descendent models that need to be evaluated to determine the next step are indicated therein. All paths terminate in any one of three kinds of bipartitions, numerically with 6:1, 5:2, and 4:3 variables. The quantitative criteria guiding this search are as in the previous searches. One considerable advantage of this algorithm is that none of the models involved contain loops and can thus be evaluated more efficiently than those that do.

Figure 41 depicts the results of reapplying the algorithm to each part of a partition of seven variables, ultimately achieving the complete decomposition into separate variables. The lattice does not show the

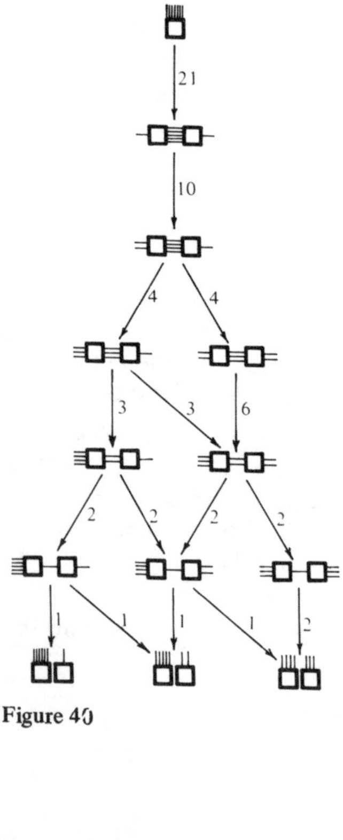

Figure 40

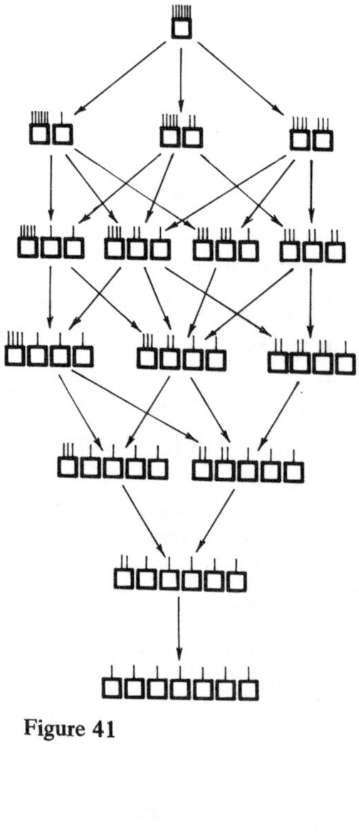
Figure 41

models that are intermediate to these partitions. For example, the whole lattice in Figure 40 is summarized as the first step of the process shown in Figure 41. The informational difference between the original data and the first bipartition expresses the interdependence between the two principal parts of that partition. Subsequent differences express additional interdependencies between the two parts of a finer partition, thus revealing a hierarchical account of interdependencies. Such differences often are interpreted as measures of communication between the two subsystems in the context of a (sub)system to which both belong. The sum of these quantities along any one path in this lattice equals the total amount of communication within the whole system, and this total is invariant to the order by which the partition was obtained.

Again, there are variations to the partitioning algorithm. For example, one may take not absolute but relative information measures—as in 4.9—as decision criteria, thus favoring partitions whose parts are similar in size. One may combine the algorithm for generating bipartitions with the one for generating regression models and achieve partitions among predictor variables, and so on.

Beyond the three kinds of implementations of the general search algorithm, note that any class of models whose structural properties can be formally stated and incorporated in a process of generating descendent models can be subjected to incremental simplifications. Researchers may want to define their own problem of exploration in these terms and follow the algorithm outlined above.

A point of caution is needed here. The number of models that can be defined and must be evaluated during explorations can become large even when only moderate numbers of variables are involved. The stepwise and incremental approach followed by the search procedure reduces the computational effort considerably. But even here computational limits are approached rather quickly. This author's computer program for confirmation handles up to 10 variables with no more than 10 values each and up to 10 components. Conant (1981) has been working on a computationally more efficient approach (which cannot be presented here).

Algebraic Techniques

These techniques go back to work done by Ashby (1965, 1969) and Conant (1976) and are known to apply only to *models without loops* (Krippendorff, 1980) and *without structural zeros*. When models do contain loops, iterative procedures are required, as discussed in Chapter 12. Algebraic techniques have the advantage of computational efficiency and lead to simple conceptualizations. We extend here some of the forms introduced in Chapters 8 and 12.

The most simple identity between entropies and the two kinds of expressions for amounts of information is

$$\mathbf{I}(m_o \rightarrow m_j) = \mathbf{H}(m_j) - \mathbf{H}(m_o) = \mathbf{T}(m_j) \qquad [14.2]$$

It does not hold for models with loops (8.3). We generalize this identity to any two models that are loopless, cover the same variables, and are related by descendency. Let $m_i = K_1\!:\!K_2\!:\!\ldots\!:\!K_f\!:\!\ldots$ and $m_j = K_a\!:\!K_b\!:\!K_c\!:\!\ldots\!:$

$$\mathbf{I}(m_i \rightarrow m_j) = \mathbf{H}(m_j) - \mathbf{H}(m_i) = \mathbf{T}(x_1) + \mathbf{T}(x_2) + \ldots + \mathbf{T}(x_f) + \ldots \qquad [14.3]$$

$$x_f \quad = K_f \& K_a : K_f \& K_b : K_f \& K_c : \ldots \text{ redundant parts eliminated}$$

$$\mathbf{T}(K) = 0$$

We also introduce a notational simplification by entering variables shared by all components of a model as subscripts:

$$\mathbf{T}(LK_1 : LK_2 : LK_3 : \ldots) = \mathbf{T}_L(K_1 : K_2 : K_3 : \ldots) \qquad [14.4]$$

which identifies variables in L as the controlling variables of $K_1\!:\!K_2\!:\!K_3\!:\!\ldots$. For example, for $m_i = ABCD\!:\!BCDE \rightarrow m_j = ABC\!:\!BCD\!:\!CE$:

$$x_1 = ABCD\&ABC : ABCD\&BCD : ABCD\&CE = ABC : BCD$$
$$x_2 = BCDE\&ABC : BCDE\&BCD : BCDE\&CE = BCD : CE$$

and

$$\mathbf{I}(m_i \rightarrow m_j) = \mathbf{H}(m_j) - \mathbf{H}(m_i) = \mathbf{T}(ABC : BCD) + \mathbf{T}(BCD : CE)$$
$$= \mathbf{T}_{BC}(A : D) + \mathbf{T}_C(BD : E)$$

wherein the two **T**-measures assess communication between A and D and between BD and E, both of which are present in m_i but absent from m_j. Equation 8.8 exemplified the application of 14.3 to communication chains. In both cases **T**-measures cover different variables. Equation 14.3 states a fundamental relationship between the **I**-measures, which have descendent models of the same covers in their arguments, and **T**-measures, which express dependencies between the variables involved in the differences between these models.

Algebraic techniques for exploration essentially decompose a total amount of information into additive quantities. These additive quantities collectively designate one or more paths through a lattice of loopless models (also see Figure 43), summarize the information losses of several intermediate models (without actually evaluating them explicitly), and thus help the researcher to find paths along which strong structures exist. Figure 42 shows the **T**-measures along the two paths between ABCD:BCDE and ABC:BCD:CE. If a quantity is insignificant, all intermediate models are not worth exploring and may be ignored in the search for an optimum. If one or more of these quantities is statistically significant, a systematic top-down search for the optimum can start with the simplest descendent model implicit in the insignificant **T**-measures. In the example, if $\mathbf{T}_C(BD:E)$ is and $\mathbf{T}_{BC}(A:D)$ is not significant, then one would initiate a search with the model ABC:BCDE.

We now state three identities and derive a fourth, all of which may be used for algebraic exploration in a lattice of loopless models. The first is the *extension to more variables:*

$$\mathbf{T}(A:B:C:D:\ldots) = \mathbf{T}(A:B) + \mathbf{T}(AB:C) + \mathbf{T}(ABC:D) + \ldots \qquad [14.5]$$

It equates the total amount of information in data $\mathbf{T}(m_{ind})$ with a series of binary transmission terms, each covering one variable more than the preceding one. The order of variables being arbitrary, numerous enumeration schemes are possible. In the three-variable case,

$$\begin{aligned} \mathbf{T}(A:B:C) &= \mathbf{T}(A:B) + \mathbf{T}(AB:C) \\ &= \mathbf{T}(A:C) + \mathbf{T}(AC:B) \\ &= \mathbf{T}(B:C) + \mathbf{T}(A:BC) \end{aligned}$$

Each identity evaluates at least one path in the lattice of loopless models between ABC and A:B:C, which bypasses all models with loops, and in this case also the models AB:BC, AB:AC, and AC:BC. (See Figure 25 for the complete lattice.)

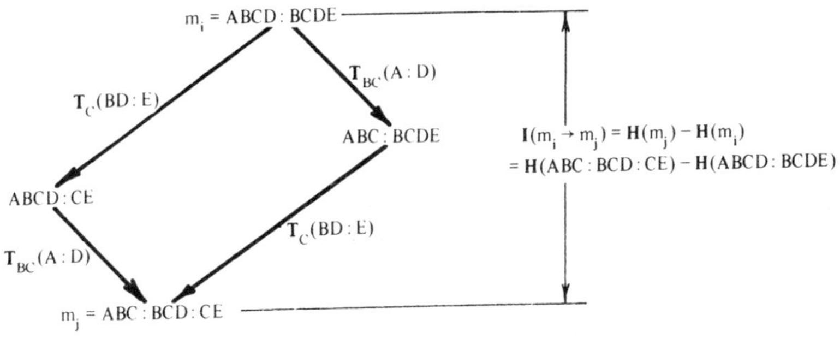

Figure 42

The second identity concerns *partitions into mutually exclusive parts:*

$$\mathbf{T}(A{:}B{:}C{:}\ldots{:}L{:}M{:}N{:}\ldots) = \mathbf{T}(A{:}B{:}C{:}\ldots) + \mathbf{T}(L{:}M{:}N{:}\ldots) + \mathbf{T}(ABC\ldots{:}LMN\ldots) \qquad [14.6]$$

It suggests that the total $\mathbf{T}(m_{ind})$ can be broken down into the sum of the amounts of information *within* each part plus the amount of information *between* these parts. This identity underlies the search algorithm for partitions and the path(s) such an identity evaluates can be envisioned by means of Figure 41.

The third identity is related to the *regression of one variable in terms of all others:*

$$\mathbf{T}(ABC\ldots{:}Z) = \mathbf{T}(A{:}Z) + \mathbf{T}_A(B{:}Z) + \mathbf{T}_{AB}(C{:}Z) + \ldots + \mathbf{T}_{ABC..}(Y{:}Z) \qquad [14.7]$$

It expresses the total amount of information between one variable, Z, and all others, ABC..., as a function of the information between Z and one other, Z and a second other controlled for by the first, and so on. Applying 4.5 to the left side and bringing the conditional entropy $\mathbf{H}_{ABC\ldots}(Z)$ in $\mathbf{T}(ABC\ldots{:}Z)$ to the other side yields

$$\mathbf{H}(Z) = \mathbf{T}(A{:}Z) + \mathbf{T}_A(B{:}Z) + \mathbf{T}_{AB}(C{:}Z) + \ldots + \mathbf{T}_{ABC..}(Y{:}Z) + \mathbf{H}_{ABC..}(Z) \qquad [14.8]$$

where $\mathbf{H}(Z)$ is the entropy in the variable Z to be explained, $\mathbf{H}_{ABC\ldots}(Z)$ is the unexplainable entropy or noise in Z, and $\mathbf{T}$ terms are the incremental contributions to $\mathbf{H}(Z)$. A stepwise regression procedure naturally follows from this equation. It would start by searching for a variable Y for which $\mathbf{T}_{ABC\ldots}(Y{:}Z)$ is minimum, then search for a variable X for which $\mathbf{T}_{ABC\ldots}(X{:}Z)$ is a minimum, and so on until a simple binary transmission term of the form $\mathbf{T}(A{:}Z)$ remains. (Proceeding from the largest value of $\mathbf{T}(A{:}Z)$ may not be advisable given that higher-order interactions would escape this measure, whereas the conditional measures use them as controls.)

Applying now the identity of regression 14.7 to each of the parts obtained from the identity of extension 14.5 gives the following account:

$$
\begin{array}{llllll}
 & \mathbf{T}(A:B) + & \mathbf{T}(AB:C) + & \mathbf{T}(ABC:D) + & \mathbf{T}(ABCD:E) + \ldots & \\
 & \Downarrow & \Downarrow & \Downarrow & \Downarrow & \\
= & \mathbf{T}(A:B) + & \mathbf{T}(A:C) + & \mathbf{T}(A:D) + & \mathbf{T}(A:E) + \ldots & [14.9] \\
 & & + \mathbf{T}_A(B:C) + & \mathbf{T}_A(B:D) + & \mathbf{T}_A(B:E) + \ldots & \\
 & & & + \mathbf{T}_{AB}(C:D) + & \mathbf{T}_{AB}(C:E) + \ldots & \\
 & & & & + \mathbf{T}_{ABC}(D:E) + \ldots & \\
 & & & & + \ldots & \\
= & \mathbf{T}(A:B:C:D:E:\ldots) & & & &
\end{array}
$$

Each of these terms represents an informational difference between two descendent loopless models that are one generation apart. These quantities partition the total amount of information into the incremental information losses along some path through the lattice of possible loopless models from m_o to m_{ind}. Again, variables can be taken in any order, and 14.9 can be used to evaluate any path through this lattice. Moreover, and inasmuch as some of these terms can be rearranged and applied to different models, a given set of terms may be shared by several such paths. Figure 43 depicts the 16 possible paths for which the terms in 14.9 can account. For simplicity, this figure represents the same **T** terms by the same kind of line and at the same angle, thus showing the different positions these terms may occupy along these paths. Finding, for

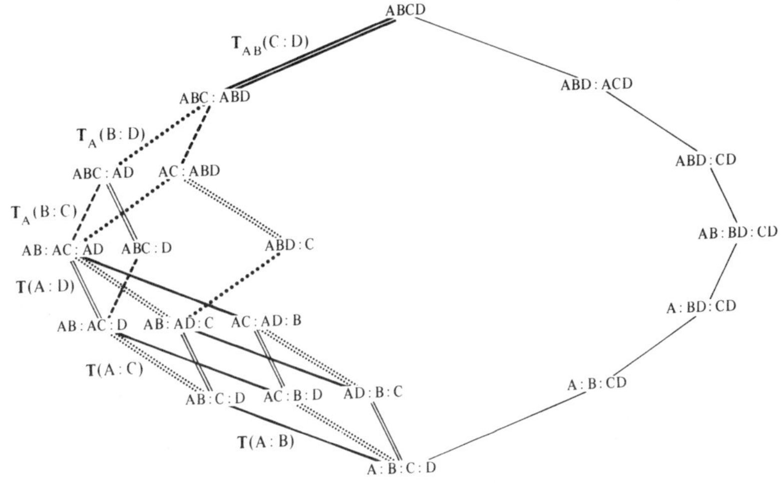

Figure 43

example, that $T_A(B{:}C)$ and $T(A{:}B)$ are significant whereas all others are not would suggest that the optimum model lies somewhere between ABC:D and AC:B:D from both of which D could be ignored as a noncontributory variable.

Even though algebraic techniques are restricted to loopless models, they do provide useful tools for exploring the complexity of multivariate data and become essential outside the computational limits for evaluating models with loops.

15. COMPARISONS WITH ALTERNATIVE APPROACHES

Network and Path Analyses

The information theory for the structural modeling of qualitative data has much in common with network analysis, path analysis, and the structural modeling approach to quantitative data: All respond to the need to make relations in multivariate data transparent. Network analysis, for example, largely starts with bivariate data, such as who talks to whom and how often, distances in space, or differences in time or in other magnitudes; aggregates such data much as graph theory does; and then identifies chains, loops, bottlenecks, centralities, and so on but is unable to consider relations of ordinality higher than two. Higher-order causes or consequences sometimes enter the path diagrams as complicating phenomena, but because its arrows link variables in pairs, the approach is basically focused on bivariate explanations of multivariate phenomena. (Try drawing a line connecting three points other than in pairs!) The coefficients of structural equation models, briefly discussed in Chapter 6, do not need to but often do express linear relations between pairs of variables and are thus similarly limiting. The information theory approach is not so restricted, however. It considers binary relations merely as a special case, Shannon's communication chain being a historical example. It routinely incorporates higher-order interactions in its models and thus enables researchers to develop and test theories—especially communication theories—of theoretically unlimited complexity.

Also mentioned in Chapter 6 is that the parameters of information-theoretical models do not rely on mathematical assumptions and forms. Whereas structural equation approaches tend to make linear assumptions or construct its models through other mathematical idealizations, the parameters of information-theoretical models are the very distributions found in the multivariate data themselves, without any simplification. It follows that any kind of relation, linear/nonlinear, unimodal/multimodal, deterministic/probabilistic, and so on, is preserved in the distributions our models generate. The information theoretical approach is hence entirely general.

Chi-Square

Chapter 11 explored the role of the maximum likelihood approximation $\mathbf{L}^2$ in providing information theory with access to the familiar χ^2 tables. All three quantities

$$\chi^2 = n \sum \frac{(p - \pi)^2}{\pi}$$

$$\mathbf{I} = \sum p \log_2 \frac{p}{\pi}$$

$$\mathbf{L}^2 = 2n \sum p \log_e \frac{p}{\pi} = 1.3863\, n\, \mathbf{I}$$

are zero when the observed probabilities p equal the expected probabilities π and increase in magnitude with increasing differences between the two. χ^2 and $\mathbf{L}^2$ are functions of the sample size n; the information **I** is independent of it.

Despite these functional similarities, a major difference is that **I** and $\mathbf{L}^2$, the latter being a mere multiple of **I**, are additive in ways χ^2 is not. In particular, differences in χ^2 values are uninterpretable, whereas many differences among information quantities yield other information quantities that can be subjected to the same tests as the quantities from which they were derived. Thus as Ku and Kullback (1974) and many others have concluded, information quantities provide researchers with an analytical flexibility unknown to χ^2 users, and information statistics are therefore often preferable to χ^2 statistics.

Another difference lies in the magnitude individual cells contribute to the two measures. Cell contributions to χ^2 are known to become unjustifiably large when expected frequencies (which appear in its denominator) are small or nearly absent. This is the primary reason why the use of χ^2 statistics calls for a minimum of five expected observations per cell (strict condition) or an average of five or more observations per cell (weak condition), which, in the context of multivariate analysis, often makes exorbitant demands on adequate sample sizes. In contrast, the log-likelihood contributions to information quantities are weighted by the observed frequencies in a cell, and each contribution is therefore proportional to this frequency (see Figure 15 for examples).

Although information measures become biased as well when samples are inadequate, they tend to overestimate the true quantities involved. In significance tests, such biases make the rejection of null hypotheses (that observed and expected probability distributions really are the same) more likely when they are true in fact and thus favor models that are more complex than necessary and include the correct model as one of their descendents. Chapter 11 concluded that in the structural modeling context inadequate sample sizes render information statistics not inappropriate but merely more conservative.

Analysis of Variance

The similarity of entropy as a measure of diversity or variety and variance was explored in Chapter 3, which suggested that entropy, implying no assumptions regarding the order or shape of the distribution in data, is the more general of the two. This argument is further strengthened by the fact that information quantities for interval data or "continuous channels" have been proposed in the original work by Shannon and Weaver (1949), whereas a converse proposal for applying the analysis of variance to qualitative data or "discrete channels" is unavailable. Despite these differences there are interesting similarities that stem from their respective logic of partitioning variation. In the analysis of variance

$$V_{total} = V + V^{A} + V^{B} + V^{AB} + V^{C} + V^{AC} + V^{BC} + V^{ABC} + \ldots \qquad [15.1]$$

where each effect is defined independent of all others—for example, V^{AB} excludes what V^{A} and V^{B} contribute and is in turn excluded from the contribution by V^{ABC}, thus accounting for the unique effect of the interaction <AB> on the criterion variable, say Z. For W predictor variables 15.1 has 2^{W} terms.

A partition of information quantities resembling 15.1 is found in 14.7, wherein the total amount of information in Z, T(ABC...:Z), corresponds to V_{total}, T(A:Z) corresponds to V^{A}, $T_{A}(B:Z)$ corresponds to $V^{B} + V^{AB}$, $T_{AB}(C:Z)$ to $V^{C} + V^{AC} + V^{BC} + V^{ABC}$, and so on. Evidently both forms are capable of accounting for the variation in one variable by partitioning others. However, the information identity 14.7 accounts for these components in groups. The reason for this property will become clear in the following comparison.

Log-Linear Modeling

Log-linear modeling (Goodman, 1972; Bishop et al., 1978) is related to information theory as well. It proposes an additive function similar to 15.1 for explaining not the variation in one variable but the frequencies in the very multivariate space it partitions:

$$\log_e n_{abc..} = u + u_a^A + u_b^B + u_{ab}^{AB} + u_c^C + u_{ac}^{AC} + u_{bc}^{BC} + u_{abc}^{ABC} + \ldots \quad [15.2]$$

where u is the average $\log_e n_{abc...}$ over all cells, u_a^A expresses the deviation from this average on account of A, u_{ab}^{AB} expresses the deviation due to AB over and above what u, u_a^A, and u_b^B express, and so on. All u terms are logarithms of various forms of cross-product ratios, and the form of this function obviously resembles that used in the analysis of variance except that it applies to individual cells.

For two reasons the ideal of 15.2 is unachievable. First, u terms are not entirely independent. Already u_{abc}^{ABC} is no longer obtainable by algebraic means because it would have to exclude the effects of u_{ac}^{AC}, u_{ab}^{AB}, and u_{bc}^{BC}, which, taken together, constitute a loop and must be evaluated iteratively. The sum of these parts does not equal the whole, which challenges the function's additivity. Second, to obtain expected frequencies, u terms cannot be zeroed arbitrarily. Bishop et al.'s "hierarchy principle" (1978: 67-68) formalizes the order in which contributions may or must be grouped, thus curbing the freedom to assemble the u terms into models that the function's notations claim.

The information theory for structural modeling provides an additive form as well:

$$\mathbf{I}(m_o \to m_{ind}) = \mathbf{I}(m_o \to m_1) + \mathbf{I}(m_1 \to m_2) + \ldots + \mathbf{I}(\ldots \to m_{ind}) \quad [15.3]$$

It partitions the total amount of information into up to $2^W - W - 1$ additive quantities, representing contributions similar to 15.1 and 15.2 except for those associated with the W single variables (which appear moved here to the left side of the expression and are contained in $\mathbf{I}(m_o \to m_{ind})$) and the overall term, which is zero. If models are immediate descendents, then each informational difference measures the contribution of exactly one interaction, just as in the analysis of variance and intended by the log-linear ideal, but it measures these always in the context of the model from which it is removed, thus implying that these contributions are ordered. The notation $m_o \to m_1 \to m_2 \to \ldots \to m_{ind}$ indicates a descendence ordering of those contributions and designates one path through the lattice of possible models. There are therefore up to as many additive functions of the form 15.3 available as there are paths through such a lattice.

On the surface, the absence of a single accounting equation and the context sensitivity of the additive quantities involved might seem disadvantageous. However, this merely recognizes Bishop et al.'s hierarchy principle. Whereas the log-linear approach postulates the ideal of a single additive function of all possible contributions and must then tell users that its terms cannot be analyzed (assembled or ignored) freely, the information-theoretical approach has built the same restrictions into its logic of structural models (see Chapter 6) and into its accounting equations that implicitly abide by this logic. With this in mind, the informational account, besides offering a summary account for *all* cells, is simpler than the log-linear approach. I surmise this difference to be also one of style: The log-linear approach grew out of the traditions of analysis. The information-theoretical approach grew out of an iterative exploration of data.

The Most Basic Reference Possible

Finally, throughout the book we stated all informational accounts with reference to models of the *same* cover. This places m_{ind} at the base of the lattices of models considered here and defines $\mathbf{I}(m_o \rightarrow m_{ind}) = \mathbf{T}(m_{ind})$ as the maximum amount of information such models can explain. It disallows the simple omission of variables and prevents an accounting of the contributions such omitted variables make. For practically all structural modeling tasks this reference is sufficient and we chose it for this very reason. However, nothing prevents an extension of the information quantities to models with *different covers* that claim no knowledge about the distribution in some (or all) variables (Krippendorff, 1981) and to state individual contributions in terms of 2^W logarithmic functions of frequencies analogous to 15.2.

$$\log_2 n_{abc..} = \log_2 \frac{n}{N_A N_B N_C \cdot\cdot} \qquad [15.4]$$

$$+ \log_2 \frac{p_a}{\frac{1}{N_A}} + \log_2 \frac{p_b}{\frac{1}{N_B}} + \log_2 \frac{p_{ab}}{p_a p_a}$$

$$+ \log_2 \frac{p_c}{\frac{1}{N_C}} + \log_2 \frac{p_{ac}}{p_a p_c} + \log_2 \frac{\rho_{abc}}{\frac{p_{ab}\, p_{ac}}{p_a}} + \log_2 \frac{p_{abc}}{\rho_{abc}} + \ldots$$

Here n is the sample size, N_A is the number of occupiable cells in A, and ρ_{abc} is the probability generated by the model AB:AC:BC (which contains a loop). $\log_2 n/N_A N_B N_{C...}$ resembles the general u term, and all other parts of 15.4 are log-likelihood ratios whose non-zero values indicate the magnitude and direction of an effect on $\log_2 n_{abc...}$. Figure 44 exemplifies this account.

Averaging the parts in 15.4 and moving the $\log_2 n/N_A N_B N_C...$ term to the left side of the identity yields $2^W - 1$ information quantities. In the three-variable case 15.4 becomes

$$\mathbf{T}(\overline{ABC}) = \mathbf{T}(\bar{A}) + \mathbf{T}(\bar{B}) + \mathbf{T}(A:B) + \mathbf{T}(\bar{C}) + \mathbf{T}(A:C) + [\mathbf{T}_A(B:C) - \mathbf{T}(AB:AC:BC)] + \mathbf{T}(AB:AC:BC) \quad [15.5]$$

where the redundancy $\mathbf{T}(\overline{ABC})$ is the informational difference between the presence and the *total absence of any knowledge* about a probability distribution in selected variables, $\mathbf{T}(\overline{ABC...}) = \mathbf{I}(m_o \rightarrow m_{max})$ generalizes 4.10, and the other **T** measures are as usual. An analysis of the Florida murder trial data in Figure 1 demonstrates the use of these forms. Figure 44 shows all models along the optimum path (as defined by the search algorithm in Chapter 14), the frequency distributions in their parameters, and the maximum entropy frequencies generated by them jointly (rounded to full integers). The meaning of m_{max} as the ultimate descendent may also become clear in the latter distribution. The race of the murderer is A, the race of the victim is V, and the outcome of the trial is O, as shown in Figure 4.

The figure also illustrates the use of 15.4 to explain the cell of 48 cases in which the murder victims are white and the perpetrators of the crime are black and sentenced to death. Its eight terms sum to $\log_2 48 = 5.5850$. Knowledge of <O>, that death penalty is rare in comparison to other outcomes, and of <AV>, that interracial violence is less frequent than intraracial violence, accounts for the largest deviations and indicates that observed frequencies are less than those assumed by the uniform distribution. Knowledge of <VO>, that death penalty is more likely when victims are white, and of < AO>, that murderers are more likely sentenced to death when they are black, accounts for increases in frequency in this cell. A third-order interaction is absent.

The figure also contains a complete account according to 15.5 of the total amount of redundancy $\mathbf{T}(\overline{AVO}) = \mathbf{I}(m_o \rightarrow m_{max}) = 1.4421$ bits. Only the third-order quantity turns out to be zero. All descendents of the model AV:AO:VO exhibit statistically significant errors and cannot be accepted as adequate models of these data. Because this simple $2 \times 2 \times 2$ example has few degrees of freedom, 15.4 and 15.5 yield essentially similar insights. This may not be so when variables involve finer distinctions and cells make very different contributions.

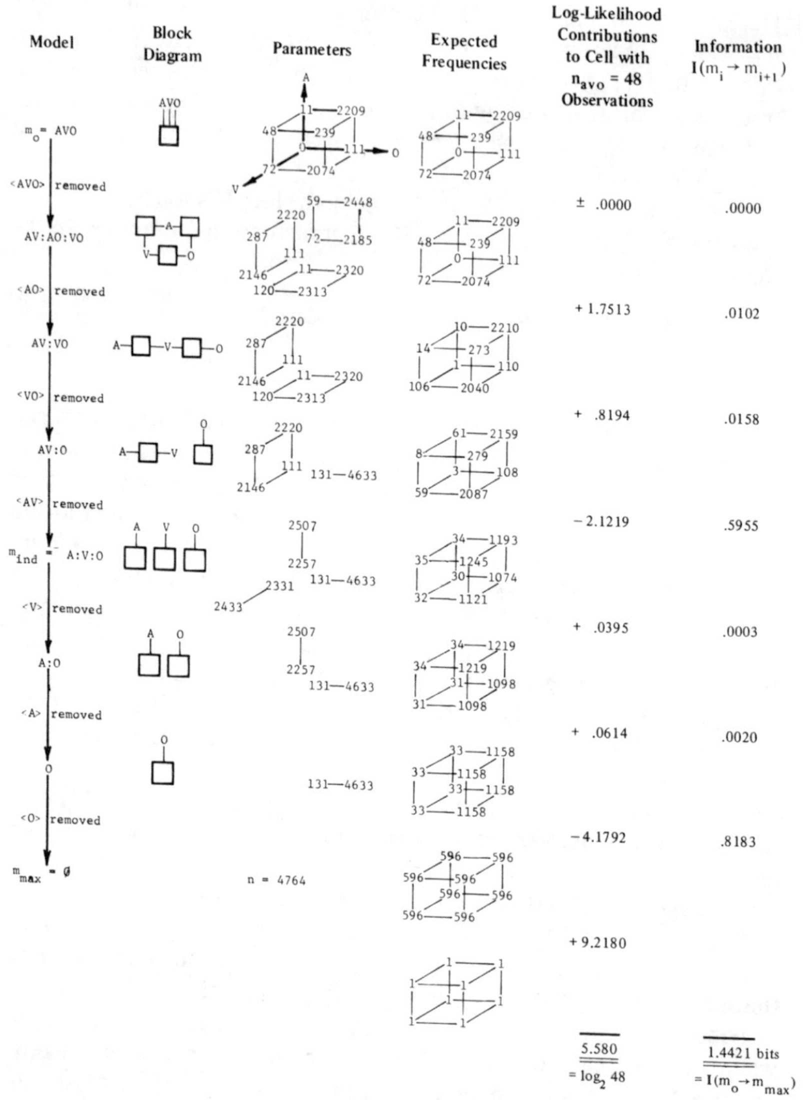

Figure 44

In conclusion, the information theory for structural modeling has aims similar to such traditional approaches as network and path analyses, χ^2 statistics, analysis of variance, and log-linear modeling but accomplishes them more elegantly, provides greater analytical power and flexibility, retains more direct touch with the (mathematically) uncontaminated data, and suggests interpretations closer to social theory, to communication theory in particular.

16. LIST OF SYMBOLS

A, B, C, ..., Z	Single qualitative variables of a multi-variate space (1)
AB, ABC...Z	Product, matrix, or table; a multi-variate space (1)
$a \epsilon A$, $abc...z \epsilon ABC...Z$	Category of value of A; many-tuple or cell of a multi-variate space (1)
df	Degrees of freedom: $\mathbf{df}_K$ in a component K (10.1); **df** in a model m (10.3); $\mathbf{df}_{m_i \to m_j}$ in interactions removed (10.2), (10.5)
H	Entropy: **H**(A) in variable A (3.1)-(3.3); **H**(ABC...Z) in a multi-variate space (3.5); **H**(m) in a model m (8.1), (12.1); $\mathbf{H}_{max}$ the largest possible value of **H** (3.4)
I	Information: $\mathbf{I}(a \epsilon A)$ selective information (2.2); $\mathbf{I}(m_i \to m_j)$ information in model m_i and absent from m_j (8.4)
K	Component of a model consisting of a variable or a product as one of that model's parameters (6)
$K_1{:}K_2{:}K_3{:}...{:}K_r$	Model, designated by its r components (6)
K_e & K_f	Variables or product shared by K_e and K_f (6)
L, M, S, $\overline{S}$	Variable or product of variables; $\overline{S}$ complementing S in ABC...Z
$\mathbf{L}^2$	Maximum likelihood approximation to χ^2 (11.1)
m	Model (6): m_i or $m_j = K_1{:}K_2{:}K_3{:}...$; m_o = ABC...Z the saturated model, the original data; m_{ind} = A:B:C:...:Z the model of independent variables; m_{max} the model of total ignorance about the distribution in ABC...Z (15.4)
N	Number of available categories or occupiable cells (2): N_A in variable A; $N_{ABC...Z}$ in a multi-variate space
n	Frequency of observations (3): n the total number or sample size; n_a in category a of A; n_{ab} in a cell of an AB-matrix or two-way table; $n_{abc...z}$ in a cell of a multi-variate space
P	Logical probability (2)
p	Observed probability (3), subscripts as for n. (Table 4.1)

ω	Maximum entropy probability generated by m_i (8), subscripts as for n
ρ	Maximum entropy probability generated by m_j (8), subscripts as for n
π	Maximum entropy probability generated by m_{ind} (4), (8), subscripts as for n
T	Information: $\mathbf{T}(\bar{A})$ redundancy in variable A (4.10); $\mathbf{T}(m) = \mathbf{T}(K_i{:}K_2{:}\ldots)$ information transmitted between components K of m (information in data but not modelled) (4.4)-(4.7), (8.2)
t	Coefficient (of association) assessing the strength of relations within a component K in the context of a model m (4.9), (13.5)
U	Uncertainty (2.1)
W	Number of variables covered by a model (14.1), denotes maximum ordinality in data when used as superscript
w	Number of variables in a component (14.1) or product, denotes ordinality when used as superscript
χ^2	Chi-square, value of a test-statistics (11), (15)
$\langle K \rangle$	Interaction: a relation involving all and only variables in K (6)
$\rightarrow$	Descendency: in $m_i \rightarrow m_j$, m_j is a descendent of m_i, and m_i is m_j's ancestor (6)
$m_i \cup m_j$	Nearest common ancestor of m_i and m_j (6)
$m_i \cap m_j$	Nearest common descendent of m_i and m_j (6)
Σ	Sequential summation, e.g., if a = 1,2,...,r then $\sum_a p_a = p_1+p_2+\ldots+p_r$
log	Logarithm function, defined by: $n = x^{(\log_x n)}$, where x is its base. The dual logarithm $\log_2$ has 2 as its base (see Figure 6); $N = 2^U$. It implies:

$$\log_x 1 = 0$$
$$\log_x x = 1$$
$$\log_x nw = \log_x n + \log_x w$$
$$\log_x \frac{n}{W} = \log_x n - \log_x w$$
$$\log_x n^w = w \log_x n$$
$$\log_y n = \frac{\log_x n}{\log_x y}$$

REFERENCES

ASHBY, W. R. (1956) An Introduction to Cybernetics. London: Chapman and Hall.
———(1964) "Constraint analysis of many-dimensional relations." General Systems Yearbook 9: 99-105.
———(1965) "Measuring the information exchange in a system." Cybernetica 8, 1: 5-22.
———(1969) "Two tables of identities governing information flows within large systems." American Society for Cybernetics Communications 1, 2: 3-8.
ATTNEAVE, F. (1959) Applications of Information Theory to Psychology. New York: Holt, Rinehart & Winston.
BENSE, M. (1956) Aesthetische Information: Aesthetica II. Krefeld, Germany: Aegis.
BERLYNE, D. E. (1971) Aesthetics and Psychobiology. New York: McGraw-Hill.
BISHOP, Y.M.M., S. E. FIENBERG, and P. W. HOLLAND (1978) Discrete Multivariate Analysis. Cambridge: MIT Press.
CHAFFEE, S. H. and D. G. WILSON (1977) "Media rich, media poor: two studies of diversity in agenda-holding." Journalism Quarterly 54: 466-476.
CONANT, R. C. (1976) "Laws of information which govern systems." IEEE Transactions on Systems, Man, Cybernetics 64: 240-255.
———(1981) "Detection and analysis of dependency structures." International Journal of General Systems 7, 1: 81-90.
DANOWSKI, J. A. (1974) "An uncertainty model: friendship communication networks and media related behaviors." East Lansing: Department of Communication, Michigan State University. (unpublished)
———and J. E. RUCHINSKAS (1979) Media Channel Entropy: Age, Media Cohort, and Periodic Effects. Research Report. Los Angeles: Annenberg School of Communications, University of Southern California.
DARNELL, D. K. (1970) "Clozentropy: a procedure for testing English language proficiency of foreign students." Speech Monographs 37: 36-46.
———(1972) "Information theory: an approach to human communication," pp. 156-169 in R. W. Budd and B. D. Ruben (eds.) Approaches to Human Communication. New York: Spartan.
DARROCH, J. N. and D. RATCLIFF (1972) "Generalized iterative scaling for log-linear models." Annals of Mathematical Statistics 43, 5: 1470-1480.
DIACONIS, P. and B. EFRON (1983) "Computer-intensive methods in statistics." Scientific American 248, 5: 116-130, 170.
FINN, S. (1985) "Unpredictability as correlate of reader enjoyment of news articles." Journalism Quarterly 62: 334-339.
GALTUNG, J. (1975) "Entropy and the general theory of peace," in J. Galtung (ed.) Essays in Peace Research, Vol. 1. Atlantic Highlands, NJ: Humanities Press.
GOKHALE, D. V. and S. KULLBACK (1978) The Information in Contingency Tables. New York: Marcel Dekker.
GOODMAN, L. A. (1972) "A general model for the analysis of surveys." American Journal of Sociology 77: 1035-1086.
KLIR, G. J. (1976) "Identification of generative structures in empirical data." International Journal of General Systems 3, 2: 89-104.
———[ed.] (1981) Special issue on reconstructability analysis. International Journal of Systems Science 9.
KRIPPENDORFF, K. (1975) "Information theory," in G. J. Hanneman and William J. McEwen (eds.) Communication and Behavior. Reading, MA: Addison-Wesley.
———(1980) "An interpretation of the information theoretical Q-measure." Proceedings of the Fifth International Meeting on Cybernetics and System Research (Vienna).
———(1981) "An algorithm for identifying structural models of multi-variate data." International Journal of General Systems 7: 63-79.
———(1982a) "A proposal for an algorithm for generating loopless or recursive models of multi-variate data," pp. 299-304 in L. Troncale (ed.) A Survey of Systems Methodology. Louisville, KY: Society for General Systems Research.

———(1982b) "Regression analysis using information theory," pp. 1007-1012 in L. Troncale (ed.) A Survey of Systems Methodology. Louisville, KY: Society for General Systems Research.

KU, H. H. and S. KULLBACK (1974) "Loglinear models in contingency table analysis." American Statistician 28, 4: 115-122.

KULLBACK, S. (1959) Information Theory and Statistics. New York: John Wiley.

LACHMAN, R., J. L. LACHMAN, and E. C. BUTTERFIELD (1979) Cognitive Psychology and Information Processing: An Introduction. Hillsdale, NJ: Lawrence Erlbaum.

LAZARSFELD, P. K. (1974) Presented during a public lecture at the Annenberg School of Communications, University of Pennsylvania, Philadelphia (March 18).

LIPSET, S. M., P. K. LAZARSFELD, A. H. BARTON, and J. LINZ (1954) "The psychology of voting: an analysis of political behavior," pp. 1124-1175 in G. Lindzey (ed.) Handbook of Social Psychology, Vol. 2. Reading, MA: Addison-Wesley.

McGILL, W. J. (1954) "Multivariate information transmission." Psychometrika 19: 97-116.

MILLER, G. A. (1955) "Note on the bias of information estimates," pp. 95-100 in H. Quastler (ed.) Information Theory in Psychology. New York: Free Press.

———(1956) "The magical number seven plus or minus two: some limits on our capacity for processing information." Psychological Review 63, 2: 81-97.

———and W. G. MADOW (1954) On the Maximum Likelihood Estimate of the Shannon-Wiener Measure of Information. Report No. TR-54-75. Washington, DC: Air Force Cambridge Research Center.

MOLES, A. A. (1960) "Ueber konstruktionelle und instrumentelle Komplexitact." Grundlagenstudien aus Kybernetik und Geisteswissenschaft 1, 2: 33-36.

———(1966) Information Theory and Esthetic Perception. Urbana: University of Illinois Press.

MONTROLL, E. W. (1983) "The entropy function in complex systems," in F. Machlup and U. Mansfield (eds.) The Study of Information. New York: John Wiley.

ROGERS, E. M. and D. L. KINCAID (1981) Communication Networks: Toward a New Paradigm for Research. New York: Free Press.

SCHRAMM, W. (1955) "Information theory and mass communication." Journalism Quarterly 32: 131-146.

SHANNON, C. E. and W. WEAVER (1949) The Mathematical Theory of Communication. Urbana: University of Illinois Press.

TAYLOR, W. L. (1953) "Cloze procedure: a new tool for measuring readability." Journalism Quarterly 30: 415-433.

———(1956) "Recent developments in the use of cloze procedure." Journalism Quarterly 33: 42-48.

THEIL, H. (1972) Statistical Decomposition Analysis. New York: Elsevier.

WATT, J. H. and R. KRULL (1974) "An information theory measure for television programming." Communication Research 1: 44-64.

WATT, J. H. and A. J. WELCH (1983) "Effects of static and dynamic complexity on children's attention and recall of television instruction," in J. Bryant and D. R. Anderson (eds.) Children's Understanding of Television. New York: Academic Press.

WELTNER, K. (1973) The Measurement of Verbal Information in Psychology and Education (B. M. Crook, trans.). Berlin: Springer Verlag.

KLAUS KRIPPENDORFF is professor at the University of Pennsylvania's Annenberg School of Communications. He holds a Ph.D. from the University of Illinois, Urbana. His interest in information theory stems from teaching and writing on systems theory and cybernetics. His concern with qualitative data arose from extensive work done with content analysis. He has published in numerous journals, co-authored The Analysis of Communication Content, *edited* Communication and Controls in Society, *and authored* Content Analysis, An Introduction to Its Methodology. *His current attention is devoted to a cybernetic epistemology for communication.*